Idealism vs. Materialism

A Philosophical Defense of Christianity

by
Allen Michael Green

Foreword by Joseph Sobran

authorHOUSE®

AuthorHouse™
1663 Liberty Drive, Suite 200
Bloomington, IN 47403
www.authorhouse.com
Phone: 1-800-839-8640

First published by AuthorHouse 4/4/2008

ISBN: 978-1-4343-7517-9 (sc)
ISBN: 978-1-4343-7518-6 (hc)

Library of Congress Control Number: 2008903213

Printed in the United States of America
Bloomington, Indiana

This book is printed on acid-free paper.

Cover illustrated by Jessica Davis

DEDICATED TO
INRI

Foreword

Joseph Sobran

This little book is that rare thing, a work of metaphysics addressed to the general reader. In essence it affirms the simple words that open the Gospel of St. John: "In the beginning was the Word."

As Allen Green points out, the modern world has adopted materialism – the doctrine that only matter exists, that the entire universe is merely physical -- as both its official and its unofficial philosophy. Most people, even the educated, hardly know, and can't even imagine, that there is any alternative way of understanding reality; the young, as C.S. Lewis says in *The Abolition of Man*, are trained to take one side in a dispute before they have even grasped that there *is* a dispute, or what it is about. Once they have been conditioned by the materialist philosophy, they have barely any more conception of a spiritual view than a clam on the ocean bed has of life on land. Yet to millions of people, this bleak and dubious philosophy has come to seem self-evident.

The word "Science," meaning the natural sciences, has usurped the authority of religion, which in turn has become a barely tolerated superstition. The theory of evolution – "the creation myth of the materialists," as Mr. Green aptly puts it – now permeates both popular and "high" culture. The child who somehow escapes it in school (and not just government schools) is sure to pick it up in other places: at home, on television, in pop music and movies. And in the print media, if he can still read. The same assumptions that animate Steven Spielberg movies about sharks and dinosaurs underlie articles in the Encyclopedia Britannica and *The New York Review of Books*. The materialist worldview has become all but inescapable. And those who reject it, though remarkably numerous, are apt to appear ignorant and eccentric.

It's a strange fact of human nature that people are usually more certain of opinions they have picked up from their environment by sheer repetition than of those they have independently reasoned out and verified for themselves. In Samuel Johnson's witty words, their beliefs "are not propagated by reason, but caught by contagion." It takes unusual strength of character to hold a belief nearly all the people around you reject.

As Mr. Green also remarks, the materialist philosophy enjoys the status, as well as all the advantages, of an established religion. The state supports it, teaches it in schools, reinforces it in myriad ways, discourages and even suppresses rival views. The principle of "the separation of church and state" (mistakenly ascribed to the U.S. Constitution) is often cited by materialists to justify excluding anything they think smacks of religion.

And yet as a philosophy, materialism is not only false, but self-contradictory. You are proving it false right now, by reading and pondering these words. At this very moment you are doing several things that no animal has ever done. Animals can't reason: they can't think abstractly, generalize, imagine things that are absent, state a proposition, and so forth. In other words, *no animal can even be a materialist.* We may as well try to imagine a gorilla becoming a martyr.

The great Greek and Christian philosophers understood this. Man, they agreed, is a rational animal, the *only* rational animal: a being with the power to reason, a free will, and an immortal soul.

This is the true Western tradition, which held sway for well over two thousand years, from the great Greek philosophers until recent times. Materialism, the denial of the spiritual, represents a cultural revolution that has taken root only since the twentieth century and still remains incomplete.

Man's dual nature, as both animal *and* spiritual, is the premise of all Shakespeare's plays, for example. They assume the immorality of the soul, God's moral order, man's capacity for honor and nobility, and much more. In Shakespeare's day atheism was rare; he created a few characters who deny the spiritual, such as Iago in *Othello*, but they are evildoers whose cynical view of human nature makes them forces of destruction. Today Iago's attitude that man is by nature a mere animal has become the ruling philosophy of Western societies.

To turn the matter around: if materialism were true, we could never know that it was true. If only matter exists, all our thoughts are merely the result of physical events in our brains. And if the events in Peter's brain differ from those in Paul's, there is no use in anyone else – Henry, say – trying to decide which one is right, because Henry will only be reporting on the events in his own brain, which carry no more weight, and have no greater authority, than those in Peter's or Paul's brain. Put otherwise, materialism makes it nonsense to speak of objective truth.

How are Homer's epics, Plato's dialogues, Dante's poetry, Michelangelo's sculpture, Newton's theories, Bach's music, Moliere's comedies, and things of this order to be explained in terms of any animal activity? Are we really expected to believe that the amoeba, given enough millennia, might develop into a creature that could write *King Lear*? At times the materialist faith becomes downright hilarious.

One of the liveliest refutations of Darwin ever written, titled *Darwinian Fairytales*, is the work of the late David Stove, an atheist philosopher. Stove doesn't even bother offering scientific evidence from the fossil record; he merely quotes Darwin himself and, using the method of linguistic analysis, shows that the theory of human evolution via a "ruthless struggle for survival" *can't possibly be true.*

Why not? Simple. Man is not ruthless. He protects the weak (starting with his own women and children), heals the sick, punishes the evildoer, honors the old, seeks justice, and so forth. Civilization could never have arisen – even the most primitive society couldn't have lasted a generation -- without a great deal of this very un-Darwinian altruism.

If Darwinism were true, as Mr. Green also points out, the evidence for it would be everywhere. Random mutations would be visible all around us. There would be no finished products. We would see at least some, and probably a great many, humans and animals in the process of evolving into something else.

But in that case, where are Nature's failed experiments and freaks? Why are these, in both the human and animal worlds, the exception rather than the rule? It isn't unusual for Darwinians to forget themselves and speak of the "evolutionary purpose" of this or that organ or instinct – when the whole idea of evolutionary theory is to eliminate purpose from Nature, substituting blind accident as the explanation for everything!

So why has modern man been hypnotized by the materialist and Darwinian account of human origins? No doubt because, as Lewis says, atheism is the supreme form of wishful thinking: we all would like to be free to sin with impunity. And it's a great relief to believe that we will never have to answer to God for the evil we do: the acts of pride, revenge, spite, greed, lust, and, yes, even the seemingly harmless vices of gluttony and sloth.

Thanks to modern politics, misnamed "democracy," we can commit many of these sins collectively; we can assign the state to kill and rob for us as we nurse our own claims of unearned "rights" and our sense of grievance and victimhood. Nowadays wars are always called "defense" by the aggressors, who can be counted on to blame the actual victims for starting or provoking them.

Most modern states covet weapons of mass murder, euphemistically called "weapons of mass destruction": nuclear weapons. The very idea of these weapons, which can annihilate tens of thousands of people in a flash, has lost its power to sicken and horrify us. We often hear the extraordinary assertion that these must not "fall into the wrong hands" -- as if any hands could be the "right" ones for them! Our propagandists assure us that the "right" hands are those of "democracies," whereas the "wrong" hands are those of "dictators."

At times one wonders if people ever listen to themselves. Could any decent human being bear to have the power to kill on such a scale? What *moral* difference could it possibly make whether he was elected by popular vote? Granted, the prospect of Kim Jong-Il's having such power is especially terrifying. But why should that power exist in the first place?

Kim's Communist regime in North Korea, which out-Stalins Stalin, is the apotheosis of materialism. It utterly denies God and mercilessly persecutes Christians, while grotesquely making a god of the deranged and dwarfish Kim himself. This makes it something of an embarrassment to the West's "liberal" materialists, but we should bear in mind that they agree with it in principle.

Materialism is a remarkably aggressive ideology; we might almost call it evangelical in its eagerness to spread its grim gospel. The materialists insist that only Darwinism be taught in the public schools. Why, we may ask, is it imperative for children to learn that they are soulless animals, whose existence ends forever when they die and rot? Even a tender-hearted atheist, you'd think, might permit them the comforting belief (even if he didn't share it himself) that their Creator loves them!

But guilt hates innocence, and the materialist wants the young to share what he regards as his own guilty knowledge. He wants them to be implicated in the sins he has embraced. This, I think, is his secret spiritual motive, and it is, though of course he would deny it, a diabolical one. Nobody, not even a child, can be spared; all must have their noses rubbed in his awful "truth."

This is why the murderous materialistic regimes that began to flourish in the last century have always hated Christianity so fervently. Communism, Nazism, and the more watered-down forms of materialist politics called "liberalism," "social democracy," and so forth, have tried, whether by overt suppression or more gradual means, to eliminate belief in God and divine revelation. Their common denominator has been the dogma of Darwinian evolution – their own perverse creation myth, in which man, through the collectivist state, denies the divine and finally reinvents himself.

Yet even materialists can't quite dispense with morality, though they deny its spiritual foundations. The pathetic result is, as Mr. Green notes, that what was formerly recognized as wrong, immoral, or evil becomes merely "inappropriate"; morality is reduced to a matter of taste and social acceptability. Fewer and fewer things can be condemned.

Thus sodomy has been elevated from a perversion to a "right," though pedophilia, for some unexplained reason, is still censured. Abortion, the deliberate killing of a human fetus, has also become a "right," allegedly protected by the U.S. Constitution. In fact "sexual freedom" is at the moral heart of materialism, which has no use for chastity, the sanctification of the human person, though even the ancient pagans venerated virginity.

The very concept of intrinsic human dignity can hardly be defended in materialist terms; no wonder a fad for "animal rights" has sprung up in recent years, since there is no essential difference between man and beast (they just happen to occupy different rungs on the evolutionary ladder).

The "sexual revolution," like various utopian political revolutions, has sprung from the materialist philosophy. And its results have been just as wretched: ruined families and lives, disease, abortion, misery, low birth rates, poverty, illegitimacy, crime, and many other pathologies. It can hardly be coincidental that the illusion of sexual "liberation" was part of the Communist Revolution that did such profound damage to Russia over the last century. Even now, after Russia has abandoned communism, abortions there vastly exceed the number of live births.

As people have become sexually "liberated" from traditional morality and family ties, they have become all the more subordinated to, and enslaved by, the state -- especially the welfare state. When the individual loses his unique identity in the web of kinship ties, he is left with a far more tenuous and abstract identity as a weak political unit, with a number instead of a name, at the mercy of an impersonal government.

But the human spirit can never wholly surrender to the arid doctrines of materialism. It will always yearn for the divine, as it always has. The materialists have been willing to concede the realm of emotions to religion, so long as we recognize their authority over the intellect; Allen Green reminds us that their claim to intellectual authority is utterly empty.

Preface

When the United States was founded the culture determined the government; now the government determines the culture. The people have no real choice. Consider the governmental campaign to normalize homosexuality and to legalize homosexual marriage. All this over the objection of the vast majority of Americans. By any measure the American people are deeply alarmed about the invasion of illegal immigrants from Mexico. However, both political parties are united in turning a deaf ear to the will of the people. To think, they call it democracy.

In a very real sense, we already live in an Orwellian universe. We are more thoroughly controlled than we know. My novel *Blind Baseball: A Father's War* was written in 1984, the famous Orwellian year. What I described in story form, was the governmental intrusion into the traditional family. With marriage redefined, we now have government marriage with the state dictating the terms of family relationships. The intrusion into the family has been devastating to the culture. Of course, the intrusion means the destruction of the family. It also means the destruction of the individual.

We really don't have public education any more. We have government schools and government universities. What a power to own! The government can make the people think anything it wants although most control is gained via an agency of ignorance. The collapse of academic standards has to be quite intentional. As the great social commentator Joe Sobran says, "They used to teach Greek and Latin in high school. Now, they teach remedial English in college."

What is most incredible to me is that the United Stated Government is deeply involved in de-Christianizing America and most people do not even realize it, especially Christians. I know, I was de-Christianized.

I was twenty years old when I transferred from a theological school to Grand Rapids Junior College. After force feeding me huge doses of existentialism, evolution and New Deal liberalism, I saw the light and declared myself to be an atheist. One of my professors mocked, "There was only one Christian and he died on the cross." The mockery was financed by taxpayer money and most of it Christian money.

The truth is that I had no intellectual defense against men and women who were well educated and very experienced in their mission. I wanted to be an educated man and paid my hard earned money, but instead I got a brainwashing. One does not expect to pay a doctor to make one sick.

The counterculture movement of the New Left claimed me. It was really a decadence movement. The virtues that built America were abandoned for sex, drugs and rock 'n roll. This was very much the logical conclusion of the New Deal. Conservatives once warned that the welfare state would end up as a police state. In many ways we are there now.

It took me 15 years to modulate from atheism to agnosticism. It took me 15 more years to come back to the faith. At ate fifty the prodigal son came back to his Father.

Many people ask "What brought you back to God?" The truth is that I really did want to know the truth and I followed the evidence wherever it lead.

The church had failed me. It did not prepare me to intellectually defend myself and thus, I was vulnerable to the assault of materialism.

Philosophic materialism is the defacto religion of the United States. It claims that everything reduces to matter. In the beginning was matter and matter alone and the great production of the universe (from inorganic to organic, to life, to conscious life, to intelligence) comes from matter.

Ultimately, materialism failed me, too. It turned out to be a sophisticated, sophomoric fraud. The great appeal of materialism is that it gives ethical license to its adherents. This license is destructive; it destroys everything it touches.

I have attempted to describe another way to view the universe. Philosophic idealism, as defined in the following pages, is the antidote to the poison of philosophic materialism.

There are thousands of disputing factions within the church. What they have in common is contained in the understanding of Idealism vs materialism. My quest is to help unify the church so it may defend itself against the great lie of materialism.

This book is self published and the author has made it available at cost, to any Christian organization who wishes to use it for fund raising and witnessing.

Call, write or email us:

Allen Michael Green

10 N. Washington St.

Ypsilanti, MI 48197

734.485.7100

<u>agreen@agreen.us</u>

If at the end of its quest, a philosophy denies reality, it is deluded. If it denies knowledge, it has lost its claim to instruct. If it denies morality, it is merely decadence trying to find respectability. If it denies God, it is simply and profoundly uninformed.

Millions have left the Christian faith without ever having heard its true message. Millions more have never been exposed to the philosophical beauty of Christian Idealism.

I challenge you, dear reader, to consider the ideas put forward in this philosophical tract. The heresy of materialism has risen to dominate the world. Everyone seems to sense that something is terribly wrong with the course of civilization but few understand exactly what it is that is destroying society.

Materialism, philosophic materialism, is the problem.

Allen Michael Green

Index

Foreword vii

Preface xvii

Chapter 1 Materialism.. 1

Chapter 2 Evolution.. 13

Chapter 3 Identity.. 27

Chapter 4 The Software of the Universe 33

Chapter 5 The Separation of State and Philosophy 45

Chapter 6 Matter Is the Creator? 57

Chapter 7 The Materialist War On The Family................ 65

Chapter 8 Does God Believe In You?..................... 83

Chapter 9 The Conditional General Amnesty.................... 87

Thirteen Books That Will Change Your Life......................... 95

Chapter 1
Materialism

It was the atheist philosopher named Ayn Rand who properly identified the starting place of philosophy. Whether they know it or not, everyone is a materialist or an idealist. This is the great philosophical divide. There is no neutrality.

There are two distinct lines of reasoning; one takes the materialist path and the other is the path of idealism.

Many people in our post-modern world are so landlocked in materialism that they are unaware of any alternatives to their point of view. They don't understand what materialism is nor do they understand where it leads; however, materialism is blindly accepted by the masses and it is the philosophy of choice of the establishment. It is as much of a religion as any religion.

Definitions are in order. Materialism starts with the premise that matter is primary and from it all things flow. The great complexity of the universe, from the inorganic to the organic, to life and finally to conscious life is reducible to matter and nothing exists apart from matter.

To the materialist, the universe is basically hardware. While materialists recognize the existence of software, such as DNA, they regard software as the product of hardware. The primacy of matter is fundamental to materialism. The entire state subsidized scientific establishment operates on this premise. The whole political apparatus of the industrialized world is philosophically married to materialism.

The question arises, "From whence did we come?" To the materialist the answer is simple. We came from matter and to matter we will return. The theory of evolution is the creation myth of the materialists. The materialist view of evolution starts with matter that evolves from inorganic to organic. From there life pops into existence and then man spontaneously appears, all from natural forces. Matter is magic.

In chapter two we will show that what is known as the Theory of Evolution is both mythological and scientifically silly. To the post moderns this statement is heresy and constitutes grounds for dismissing the idea out of hand. However, we challenge the reader to consider the heresy of idealism.

Some materialists pay lip service to the possible and theoretical existence of God, but only to placate the provincials. If God is remote and out of the picture, all that is left is matter and materialism wins by the default.

Materialism and idealism do not mix. The universe is primarily one or the other. What is idealism? Idealism believes in the primacy of Intelligence. Intelligence precedes the existence of matter. In fact, Intelligence is the software of the universe and is evident everywhere. DNA is an example; however, more fundamentally, software is imprinted on the atom itself. If software didn't come first, hardware wouldn't know how to form. More will be said about idealism later. Materialism believes in the primacy of matter. Idealism believes in the primacy of Intelligence. Materialism believes the hardware proceeds software. Idealism believes that software (Intelligence) precedes hardware.

Consider the modern computer. Intelligence is encoded or impressed into registers, discs or tapes, et.al. One cannot see the software, its existence can only be inferred. However, who can deny that the computer, unaided by intelligence, can function at all? The software comes before the hardware. In fact, to operate, the hardware has to be engineered to accept instructions from the software. The computer is primarily software and secondarily hardware. The idealist view is that this is an analogy to life itself. Intelligence is primary to matter, giving it form and then using its form to impress itself onto matter. The most spectacular example is the DNA molecule. The materialists offer bizarre theories of how such a molecule could evolve but good science they do not have.

Consequences of Materialism

Materialism says that we must all be brave about death. Death, eternal death, is inevitable and death is the end of the road. If this state of affairs seems unappealing materialist tell us that at least it is "realistic." How "realism" is offered as a viable consolation for eternal death is beyond me. The more "real" eternal death is, the more absurd life becomes. What a depressing thought it is to lay down everything one has come to cherish. All that work and devotion for nothing. This is what materialism is selling.

Dostoyevsky said that "If there is no God all things are permissible." The materialist sees opportunity in such a universe. He may do anything he wishes knowing that there is no enforcement of any moral law. On the other hand, when others discover that they, too, are not bound by moral law then it becomes a free-for-all. Each man is the natural prey of other men. Such is the state of the contemporary world.

It is not an accident that the great mass murderers of the last century were materialists. Hitler, Mao, Pol Pot, Stalin and others were all materialists. In fact, Marxism teaches a special form of materialism called *dialectic materialism* and used it to justify the murder of millions. Why not, given the premise, the conclusion is logical. There is no authority to answer to and thus, man may realize any passion and may pursue any lust. That some will take this to its logical conclusion is inevitable and why shouldn't they? If omnipotent matter is all there is, then the only thing that restrains men from becoming moral monsters is sentiment, conformity or social subjectivism. Those possessed of strong passion hardly view such fluff as obstacles. If a person doesn't value your life and you are in his way, why shouldn't he cut your throat? The materialist has no convincing answer.

If some desire to impose tyranny why shouldn't they? If it means the death of others, well they are only made of matter. Eventually they will die anyway, so why not facilitate the process? In the materialist myth of evolution haven't they called life the "struggle for existence" and "the survival of the fittest?" How much clearer could they be? Here is materialism without the fig leaf. Here is its manifesto plainly stated and it means exactly what it says.

Why, exactly, shouldn't some men enslave others? The notion of justice and injustice is a moral idea that is based upon a moral equation. Man's life is valuable because the Divine Intelligence, God, has declared it to be of value. To take a life is unjust, murder, and invites the retribution of God.

If one cannot reasonably believe in God then how does one reasonable believe in society? What a poor "god" society is. On what basis does society declare one act "just" and another act "unjust?" Upon its own authority and self-declared worth? But that is precisely the problem. What if another society does not see it that way? What if another society wants to conquer, loot and enslave? In a materialist universe there is absolutely no reason to refrain from doing so. All things are permissible, including the worst crimes against humanity. In fact, under the materialist doctrine of the survival of the fittest, the victim is automatically the criminal. His crime is weakness.

To be sure, tyranny invites armed rebellion and men will, and do, go to war. Brute force and fraud are the ultimate arbiters in a materialist world. The next time you see state sponsored propaganda extolling the virtue of evolutionary materialism, please realize who sponsored the gulags, concentration camps and mass exterminations of the last century.

More Implications of Materialism

Why shouldn't men lie to one another and steal and cheat? Who is to say that anything is wrong with the sickest of human perversions? There are no satisfactory answers in a materialist universe. There is the recognition that if one violates the trust of another, then trust is broken. Morality does have a practical side. How could society have a banking system if banks routinely pilfered accounts? Trust is necessary for people to cooperate and cooperation is necessary for society to function. These are all practical values but in a materialist universe, if someone wants to destroy society, their point of view is as valid as its opposite. All things are permissible. The people who don't understand this are the exploitable suckers, and they operate under a naïve morality that makes them easy prey.

A Bandwagon Effect

As more and more people march to the beat of the materialist drum, we see materialist morality increasingly reflected in the arts and popular culture. Many books have chronicled the lamentable social decay seen everywhere. Many have attempted to identify the problem. The problem is philosophical. We are witnessing the results of materialism in society, in individuals all around us and in ourselves. Surf though the channels and you will see two dominant themes of the materialist age, pornographic sex and pornographic violence. That's popular culture. The fine arts are hardly a step above.

Sex is a drug and violence is an amplifier. A materialist has nothing to live for except cheap thrills and cheap victories. Who are they – they do not know. To what purpose do they live? The satisfaction of their desires? What do they desire? They don't really know; sex, drugs, status, power, money, dominance. Each materialist mixes his own cocktail and drinks himself into a stupor.

The Materialist Attempt to Construct Morality

Was Adolf Hitler merely inappropriate? There are many kinds of materialists and they argue about many things, but they tend to be united in some areas. In an attempt to form some kind of rules of civilization the materialists offer us "appropriate" and "inappropriate" behavior. There is no "right" or "wrong." There is behavior that is merely "appropriate" and "inappropriate." This is morality by opinion polls. Whatever the majority can agree upon is "appropriate." Thus, we conclude that the great German sponsored genocide of WWII was "appropriate," because a majority of Germans felt it to be so. If there is no God, exterminating Jews is completely appropriate and any society can do anything as long as it can muster a majority. If materialists think that their silly little concept of "inappropriate" represents a barrier to the burning passions of ambitious men, they are naive. All things are permissible including the destruction of nations. If someone is in a bad mood, why shouldn't they press the red button?

It means exactly what it means. Better that virgins weep than that we should deny our lust. If you don't think that materialism doesn't work itself down to the man in the street, think again. Serial killer Ted Bundy once said, "What difference does it make to the world if there are a few more or less people." In a materialist universe, he's right. The materialist understands that one day omnipotent matter will crush mankind in the extinction of the solar system. Extinction comes for each individual person too, and in the face of death there is little reason not to go out in a flame of glory. Why not climb to one's success over the dead bodies of ten million people or, ten or twenty women? All things are permissible.

In days gone by I used to go to my children's school and object to the teaching of "subjectivism" in the form of "values clarification." Supposedly the children were to determine their own subjective conclusions about morality and all other subjects, based on the clarification techniques presented by educators. I objected to the school, pointing out that children could come to any conclusion and any behavior on the basis of subjectivism. In recent years students commenced murdering their classmates and teachers. Apparently, after they had their values clarified they decided to murder others. All things are permissible. Ideas can be dangerous. If the subjective state of a teenager's mind concludes that murder and suicide are appropriate, who or what could possibly contradict them? Subjectivism is one form of materialist epistemology.

The Twin Pillars of Philosophy

Metaphysics and epistemology are the twin pillars of all philosophy. Metaphysics asks what is the nature of the universe and epistemology asks what is the nature of knowledge? Is there something to know and how do I know what I think I know? Materialism is a philosophical con game claiming in one moment to have certain knowledge and in the next moment claiming that there is no such thing as certainty. When it finds it convenient to deny knowledge, it claims knowledge is subjective (whatever you think it is), socially subjective (whatever society says it is) or relative (having no existence of itself, being merely dependent on one's point of view). Some contend that there is nothing to know (a metaphysical argument). Some contend that there is something to know but we cannot know it (a combination argument). Some contend that there is something to know and we can know it, but it is insignificant. There are numbers of ways materialism denies certainty.

Against its enemies, materialism claims certainty. Scientific knowledge is certain and the engineering marvels that flow from it proves that matter is all there is. Scientific and engineering knowledge may not be ultimate knowledge, but at least it's practical knowledge and it pays the bills. Anyone who disputes this is an idiot. Thus, materialism takes credit for all scientific and engineering progress, and who can deny the success of this practical kind of knowledge. In fact, it is the only universally accepted form of knowledge. The belligerence and bigotry of materialism emerges as it inflicts its creation myth on others. Man evolved from rocks and anyone who disagrees is stupid.

Thus it is that materialism denies certainty and proclaims certainty at the same time. Materialism plays epistemology both ways. Nothing is certain; however, materialism is certain, dogmatically certain. There are no absolutes proclaims the materialist at one moment. In the next moment the materialist scolds opponents for their point of view, presumably because there are absolutes not being observed. If there are no absolutes, we are all deluded and there is no point in dispute. If there are absolutes, then materialism needs to stand still and debate its moving position. If there are absolutes of knowledge, then materialism is dishonest in touting subjectivism, social subjectivism, relativism and all epistemologies that deny certainty. If there are absolutes of knowledge, perhaps there are absolutes of morality, something materialists hotly deny. Materialism is a philosophical con game; heads we win and tails you lose.

Materialism's great success is contained in the fact that it came to power without ever identifying what it was. Furthermore, its competitor, Christian idealism, did not know what it was or what to call it. Materialism never identified itself. It merely negated Christian idealism. If in the same breath materialism can deny knowledge and in the next proclaim that it holds a monopoly on knowledge, then what is this philosophy dressed in contradictions?

Materialism Unmasked

Consider what is taught in government schools. Students are routinely taught that there are no absolutes. However, if anyone challenges the teaching of evolution the materialist will declare that his creation myth is certain, containing absolute knowledge. So much so, that it (materialism) is justified to suppress alternate points of view. Again, materialism is a shameless philosophical con game and it plays epistemology both ways.

If at the end of its quest a philosophy denies reality, it is deluded. If it denies knowledge, it has lost its claim to instruct. If it denies morality it is merely decadence trying to find respectability. If it denies God, it is simply and profoundly uninformed.

The nations of the world are under the spell of materialism. In its name atrocity is sold as benefaction. Exploitation is sold as freedom and tyranny abounds. Without truth there is no peaceful way for men or nations to resolve disputes and so we will proceed into war, endless, unspeakable war. But all things are permissible in a materialist universe, and we will find out exactly the true depth of materialist depravity. The materialists think they can hold a belly full of contradictions and not incur the wrath of reality. They are profoundly mistaken and they will bring retribution upon us all.

Chapter 2
Evolution

Evolution is the creation myth of the materialist. We got here somehow and the materialist says that we are solely the product of natural forces. Materialists love to wrap themselves in the mantle of science and then posture, pose and pontificate. They are the possessors of knowledge and everyone else is a fool. There is nothing scientific about evolution.

To endlessly assert something is true does not constitute proof nor is it even necessarily evidence. Materialism is the established religion of the United States and materialists enjoy the privileges of government largess, which regularly finances their preposterous point of view in media programming and in public (government) education. Evolution is a theory that corrupt men leap at and stupid men fall for.

Evolutionists Reliance of Megaluck

Evolution is a theory that claims that nature, through the novel mechanisms of chance and dumb, blind luck, has thrown a trillion sevens in a row to produce the universe and planet earth. Thereafter, nearly a billion life forms emerged and evolved by the agency of natural selection. Mutation presents a change in an organism which is selected for or against by nature in the struggle for existence. Suddenly, all the neophytes are on their knees pledging their eternal loyalty to the god of materialism. But for their sake, we will point out the insurmountable problems of this silly theory.

First, before the existence of life all the components of life had to come together at the right place, at the right time. Atoms do not die, so there was no method to select for or against a random change. Thus, the agency that produced all the preconditions of life was, per Bertrand Russell, the "random collocation of atoms." Translation: dumb, blind luck. To engineer the preconditions of life requires a string of compatible accidents larger than the human mind can conceive, a number larger than all the electrons in the known universe. The materialists would have us believe in the existence of megaluck. They offer this organizing principle of the universe without mathematical proof or experimental testing. The concept of megaluck sounds like an answer, but it is no answer. Megaluck is silly and it's unworthy of one moment of serious consideration. This really is the end of the line for the evolution story. The debate is over. However, we continue.

Of the megaluck theory we would ask a few questions. The materialists say that "Given an infinity of time the least probable thing becomes a certainty." What a silly argument. This sort of parlor room debating trick is offered as an explanation. Things do not engineer themselves. Luck does not chain itself into an infinite string to produce worlds. The opposite is true; there is a ruthless principle of reversion to the mean. Flip a coin a million times and the closer it comes to an absolute 50/50 split between heads and tails. The materialists contend that nature can produce heads, by accident, long enough to produce the myriad preconditions of life. The materialists merely assert their silly idea and divert to another subject. They offer us no scientific proof of the law of megaluck.

Hyper-complexity and Super-miniaturization

Thus, we come to another favorite parlor room debating trick employed by the materialists. The materialists make arguments that depend upon the ignorance of the audience. Biologic life is complex beyond belief. It has super-miniaturized biotechnologies that are absolutely confounding. It is the problem of super complexity that the materialists wish to ignore. It is the problem of complexity from which the materialists wish to divert. If life were a simple thing, science would have created it long ago. Aided by the best minds in the world and unlimited resources, the scientific establishment cannot create one living cell. The reason is simple; it is because a single living cell has Byzantine complexity, so much so that its complexity cannot be accounted for on the basis of luck. If trained scientists can't create a living cell, how could dumb blind luck do the job? If science could create life, then the materialists would be jumping up and down on the grave of God. Imagine a microscopic living machine that has, counting processes, about a million parts. To defy imagination, it can replicate itself. Per microbiologist, Michael

Denton, "all the information to specify an organism as complex as man weighs less than a few trillionths of a gram. Of a billion different plant and animal organisms, their **genetic information can be fit into an object the size of a grain of salt.**" Materialists cannot account for this complexity and do not want to dwell on the subject. Thus, they divert the debate.

The Problem with Natural Selection

That the materialists believe that life created itself in Darwin's pond is not science. It is just assertion. Before life, natural selection did not exist to guide the hand of evolution; and as if this were not a big enough problem, natural selection could not possibly produce anything but adaptive changes. Here is the reason. Mutations directed toward changing an organism can be looked at as a blind experiment that the environment either accepts or rejects. The gross selection device is <u>**all**</u> or <u>**none**</u>, <u>**life**</u> or <u>**death**</u>. If the mutation is good, then the organism is blessed with continued life and vice versa. This silly argument wallows in a major assumption.

Does nature's mutational experiments happen one at a time in a "series" or do they happen simultaneously, in "parallel?" If nature's experiments were in a series, then there has not been possibly enough time for evolution to have happened on planet earth. Thus, nature must be producing hundreds of mutational experiments at the same time, parallel experiments. How, exactly, does a gross selection device like <u>**life**</u> or <u>**death**</u> select a good mutation when they are surrounded by thousands of bad mutations? Of course, there are many more bad mutations than good, because accidental mutation dictates that the vast majority of mutations must be bad mutations. The conclusion is somewhat anticlimactic. The entire edifice of evolutionary theory collapses because it has no mechanism to make it work and never did. Either nature's experiments are in series or they are in parallel. For numerous reasons they can't be in series. In parallel, nature cannot differentiate between good and bad mutations with only a gross selection device of **live** or **die**. The evolution theory collapses.

Evolution Stopped Evolving

Let us consider some other problems of the evolutionary theory. Unless evolution is no longer operative, which would require some tall explaining, it must be alive and well and around us conducting experiments. In fact, if evolution is true, we would expect that the human body must have new organs coming and old organs going. In fact, the materialists used to claim that the body had some 300 "vestigial" organs, organs in evolutionary atrophy. Examples included the pituitary gland, the pineal gland, the thalamus gland, tonsils, the coccyx (tailbone) among others. As I said, the materialist depends on the ignorance of its audience. It turns out that materialists were wrong. There are no vestigial organs. Nor are there any "incipient" organs, organs rising in the experimental stage. For some mysterious reason nature seems to have stopped its experiments. We need to hear some scientific reasons why this should be so.

Irreducible Complexity

Microbiologist Michael Behe, poses the problem of simultaneous and irreducible complexity. For a biological machine to work it needs all its primary parts to be assembled and functioning at the same time or it doesn't work. For example, a blood based circulatory system carries nutrients to cells and waste products to filtering organs. The circulatory system needs to have one additional system built in from the first day, the blood clotting mechanism. Blood clotting involves a very complex chemical circuitry that turns clotting on and off at exactly the right time. Too much clotting and you're dead. Too little or no clotting and you bleed to death. The clotting mechanism must have taken millions of years to evolve via mutations and natural selection. That means that every organism that had blood was a hemophiliac and bled to death before reaching adulthood. Maybe they got lucky and never cut themselves. Materialism depends so heavily upon luck. Thus, we request a scientific explanation for this chicken-or-egg conundrum. How exactly did animals live as hemophiliacs? There are many examples of simultaneous and irreducible complexity. Engineering students understand that a complex machine is really composed of many smaller machines that provide crucial functions for the general machine to work. A car may have all its parts but if it has no electrical system to deliver spark at exactly the right time to the cylinders, the car doesn't work. A car has perhaps a trillionth of the complexity of a single celled creature. All the parts must be assembled and operational at the same time or we have no living cell.

The complexity is irreducible and simultaneous and there is no way that nature can produce complexity with a minimum complexity that is simultaneous. The only way nature could perform such a function is if some sort of software exists in elements, compounds, organic compounds, amino acids, proteins et.al, directing simultaneous construction of multiple sub-assemblies that are all orchestrated in a final simultaneous final assembly. If such software exists, where did it come from?

Where Did Photosynthesis Come From?

Consider the kingdom of plants? All plants depend upon the process of photosynthesis for their energy production. The chemical circuitry of photosynthesis is complex indeed. To be able to change sunlight into chemical energy as a power source is no easy feat. To top it off, the entire process had to come into existence fully formed, all at one time, or there was no energy production. Little parts could not have evolved piecemeal over millions of years. Photosynthesis had to come into existence in a single generation and flawlessly operate, in every subsequent generation, without shutting down for repairs. To contend that dumb, blind matter, could do this all on its own is to believe in dumb, blind miracles.

The Problem of the Whale

The evolution story takes us from inorganic matter to organic matter to the first cell, to multiple cellular creatures, to fish, amphibians, to reptiles, to mammals, to man. How whales (mammals) ended up back in the ocean is a real problem for the evolutionist. Why would a creature go to all the evolutionary effort to adapt to land and then change its mind and go back to the sea? It had to move its nostrils from its face to the back of its head. Exactly how did nature pull off that feat and a thousand others? Live birth in the ocean is no easy task. How did that evolve along with special underwater nipples for nursing calves? How did the whale change its pelvic girdle from land use to water use, while not destroying its ability to give live birth? The materialists have no idea and offer nothing but silly sophomoric nonsense.

The DNA Molecule

Consider the DNA molecule, which regulates the activities of the cell through the creation of proteins? (Proteins are complex molecules that do work. Each protein may be regarded as a machine that does specific work.) The DNA also performs the magic of reproducing itself along with the whole cell. The DNA molecule has some 4 billion parts. It is the most complex software in the known universe and the materialists claim that it evolved slowly over a couple billion years.

The equation is reproduce or die. A species cannot miss a single generation. Exactly, how did DNA come into existence with the ability to make copies of itself? There is excruciating detail and complexity implied in the reproductive ability. And yet, materialists boldly assert without benefit of science that an accident did it. The only thing more stupid than that is that the public buys it, even though it runs contrary to common sense and scientific scrutiny.

Which Came First: Microbes or the Immune System?

There are many more difficulties with the materialist creation myth. Consider the conundrum of the microbe versus the immune system. Which came first the microbe or the immune system? If the microbe came first, then how did animal life survive? During the millions of years it took to evolve immunity the host was defenseless against the vector. On the other hand, if the immune system came first how is it that nature anticipated and responded to a problem that did not exist?

The Conundrum of Flight

How exactly did nature know that flight was possible and commenced evolutionary experiments to engineer a wing? During the millions of years of blind experimentation it took to create a wing, the bird had appendages that could neither clutch nor fly.

It appears that sometimes nature selects mutations that have no survival advantages at all in favor of an adaptation that will only exist in some remote future. To complicate things, the wing had to have been invented four times in three different kinds of creatures; insects, birds and bats (which are mammals). Where in the fossil record are the millions of evolutionary wing failures? No such record exists.

It would not do any good for a creature to be able to fly if it could not take off, land and return from where it started. To do so requires complex avionics. Consider the size of the brain of a fly and yet it can navigate and negotiate the complexities of flight. It can even land upside down on a surface, something the United States Air Force cannot do. Thus it is, that nature had to evolve a set of complex airfoils, composed of high tech materials and specialized advanced electronics (avionics) at the same time. How, exactly, did dumb blind nature know that flight was possible and that flight was only possible with a complex guidance system? Nature must have intelligence to do all that.

Hackel's Embryonic Hoax

It had already been proven a lie when it was taught to me in college by a professor with a Ph.D. in biology. Ontogeny recapitulates phylogeny; the development of the embryo retraces the evolution of the species. Because, according to the theory, we all had a common ancestor, embryos of different species bear striking resemblance in early stages of development. All of this was a fantastic scientific lie. Ernest Hackel, a 19th century Darwinist, falsified his drawings. The very small may not show much differentiation unaided by a microscope, but the microcosm is exquisitely complex and when viewed with the aid of a powerful microscope, every species has a distinct identity. For many decades science had known all this, but allowed the textbook to transmit the lie of Ernest Hackel.

The Piltdown Hoax

For forty three years, in the early part of the twentieth century, the scientific community was joyously jumping up and down on the grave of God. They had irrefutable proof of the missing evolution link between man and ape. His name was "Piltdown Man "and he was an archeological forgery. Nine hundred men did their Ph.D. theses on Piltdown Man and proceeded to spread the gospel of materialism to the uttermost parts of the world. The evolutionary creation myth has nothing to do with good science and everything to do with sham science. Materialism is a godless religion and it is all very emotional, winning converts to the materialists' faith. In modern textbooks there is never a single reference made to this forty three year scientific hoax. Science is owned by the materialist establishment. It routinely lies and covers up its lies.

The Problem of Intermediates

Consider the fossil record. If evolution were true, we would anticipate that intermediate fossil remains would positively trace back from man to ape, to our common reptilian ancestor, to amphibians, to fish, and so forth. No such fossil lineage exists for any species on earth. It isn't as if science hasn't tried. The fossil record has no intermediates. It is a scientific lie by omission. This glaring contradiction is never discussed in textbooks and an undergraduate would never know there was a problem with the fossil record.

Nebraska Man

Have you heard of "Nebraska Man?" From a single tooth great extrapolation was made to herald a new record of man's antiquity. Science is so starved for evolutionary evidence that it jumps at anything. Nebraska Man turned out to be the tooth of a pig. At the famous "Scopes" trial a pig tooth was entered into evidence as proof of the evolutionary theory.

Where Is The Law of Increasing Order?

Evolution is a theory that presupposes a law of nature that increases order and complexity. So we ask, where is the law and where are the equations? This great law of nature must be akin to the law of gravitation which is quantifiable with a host of equations discovered by Sir Isaac Newton. But alas, there is no law of increasing order. In fact, the opposite is true.

There are two great laws of nature. One, the law of conservation of energy, says that energy can only change its form but can never be created or destroyed. The second great law of science says that in every material interaction a small amount of energy is lost. The universe is said to be headed into heat death. This law is the second law of thermodynamics and is alternately called the Entropy Law, the law of increasing disorder.

Everything in existence is subject to the corruption process. Entropy is easy to see; merely look upon the wrinkles in a man's face and you will see entropy at work.

Entropy is the great gradient of nature. Everything that lives must die. Everything is wearing out. Everything that exists is corrupting and goes to its death. Evolution contends that there is a countertrend, that nature is increasing in complexity with respect to the genetics of living species. How, exactly, evolution is able to overcome the gradient of entropy is a mystery. There is no science to back up the claim. It is said that in a closed energy system, like our sun and earth, a countertrend can occur. If it is true, such a closed energy system has not halted the accumulating wrinkles on my face.

The scientific law of entropy contradicts the claim of the materialists that nature grows in complexity. If the materialists are correct, then there must be some great law of nature subject to the rules of scientific quantification. But alas, the materialists are empty- handed.

The materialist came to power promising that down the road science would produce the evidence of evolution. The evidence mounts to show the opposite. The evolutionary theory is crucial to the materialists. If we did not get here by the accidental random forces of nature, we have to go back to square one and look at the only other viable possibility, that the universe exists by design and that there is a Great Designer.

Chapter 3
Identity

The materialists are cocksure they understand the nature of dead matter. The materialist, especially scientific materialist, is positive of its declarations of the nature of the universe. Materialism is confident of its creation myth and it is confident that it sees what it thinks it sees. So much so that others are not allowed to express their point of view.

Let us consider the very heart of scientific materialism and the law of identity.

The law of identity says that a thing is a thing. A equals A. Implicit in every thought is the identity of objects and concepts. In any sentence a subject is modified by a predicate. Thus, a tree is green. A = An attribute of A.

More properly, A is defined thus:

A = The unity of all attributes of A, even if the attributes are not yet known.

And we have:

Entropy = A process causing degenerative change which is an attribute of all things which consistently changes all things. It is the identity destroyer.

The ancient Greek philosopher, Heroclitus, observed that everything is in a state of "flux." Everything is changing from moment to moment. Heroclitus said, "A man cannot enter into the same river twice." Our senses may present the illusion that the river is not changing from moment to moment but our reason says that it must be changing. Merely fast forward fifty years and an old man enters the river. Fast forward a thousand years and the river is gone and the material of man's body has been reabsorbed in the material background of nature. It appears that the same man cannot enter the same river twice.

Entropy destroys identity. Entropy destroys the identity of all entities that possess identity. Everything is subject to different rates of entropy. From the view of a great amount of time, we see things appear and vanish into the background of brute matter from which they came; ashes to ashes and dust to dust.

What then is the identity of a thing? Each thing appears to have a specific identity. Is identity only identity for a moment in time? Is a tree the unity of all its known and unknown attributes, including the attribute that destroys its identity, the attribute that makes it susceptible to entropy? Where is this moving, changing identity that moves to its demise with total inevitability? Even the granite mountain will die.

The tree is the subject and exists in reality. Should a philosopher deny this, let a tree fall on him and his argument disappears. If we speed up time, we see a tree born. We see it mature. We see it die and decay so fully that it is impossible to know it ever existed. At every moment in time, the tree is a different tree. What is it that science thinks it sees? In metaphysical reality, there is only an **implied identity**. It moves, it changes and it is illusive. It acts in contradiction to what it is. A thing should be what it is but a thing that constantly changes and changes toward its inevitable demise is not a thing to hang one's philosophical hat on. What exactly is it?

This moving target in reality provides the base of merely a practical definition; a tree is the unity of all its known and unknown attributes, even though they change their identity. The problem is further confounded because we regard trees as fungible when they, like men, are individuals, no two being the same. There is dysfunctional functionality in the materialist definition. A tree is a tree. When one is gone another replaces it and we refer to the new tree as the old tree. In this whole materialist mess we see that the tree is yet to be defined. Where exactly is its identity? If identity changes what is it that is being identified?

If entropy did not exist, then identity would be fixed. According to the Christian Idealist view, God cursed the "ground," the "periodic chart" (i.e. the very elements). Illusion was thus introduced into metaphysical reality. There was a time when identity was fixed because entropy did not exist.

The human mind craves a fixed identity. If identities are not fixed, due to entropy, then all we can do is take a snapshot of a never-ending stream of changing identities and hope that it is something to which we can cling.

If man looks to matter to define his reality, he is doomed to walk a labyrinth of deception. As long as entropy exists, all material identities are transient and undefinable. These identities contain the illusion that there is a fixed identity when there isn't.

Scientific naturalism or scientific materialism believes that matter is all there is and that nature is sufficient to explain itself. The law of identity is assumed and employed in all scientific observations and statements. The law of identity is assumed and employed in every single thought of man. However, as we stated there are great problems with the law of identity because entropy destroys identity. **Science sees implied identity and thinks it sees fixed identity**. This is the great and fundamental illusion of life.

Identity is not derived from matter. Identity is the software and it has been impressed upon matter but it can never be seen, only inferred. Identity is inferred.

Materialists believe in the primacy of matter and so they believe identity is contained in and derived from matter. To the materialist, the universe is fundamentally metaphysical. The idealist believes in primacy of intelligence. To the idealist the universe is fundamentally epistemological. Intelligence is the software impressed in matter. What is an identity that is constantly changing? There is nothing in materialism that can answer the question because it believes that identity comes from matter.

The idealist too, believes in identity. The tree really is a tree. However, its true identity can only exist in the software, in the spiritual side of the universe. The universe is not metaphysical. The universe is fundamentally epistemological, knowledge, not matter. Matter merely holds the form of identity for a moment in time. True identity is not subject to change. A equals A permanently. The enforcer of identity, the thing that makes a thing what it is, is the Intelligence of God. The concept tree is impressed on a material platform just as intelligence is impressed into a DNA molecule, a material platform. The platform corrupts, the concept is eternal.

Let us return to the tree. The DNA of the tree informs matter how to take form into a living plant that is unlike any other. The DNA informs the growth process, maintenance and repair. The DNA informs the tree how to reproduce its kind. The DNA is the software and it performs the miracle of gathering matter and transforming it into a living tree. The platform of matter is transient and subject to corruption through entropy. Only implied identity can be seen in matter. True and fixed identity comes from dimensions science has not yet discovered. Intelligence precedes matter and identity comes from intelligence. What intelligence? Why, God's, of course.

This may seem odd and it is. However, how the universe could possibly exist is odd, under any theory. The materialist view is that random chance constitutes a defacto intelligence capable of creating the universe. Not only is this odd but it is silly.

Given the idealist view of the universe, science is capable of doing all that it now does. However, idealism opens the doors of opportunity to explore a reality that science has hitherto not anticipated. Science is landlocked in matter and, as such, has foreclosed its understanding.

Chapter 4

The Software of the Universe

The entire animal kingdom is loaded with examples of biological programming, software. Within each body are many sets of programs. The body has a program to heal a wound, digest food, control acidity, clot a bleeding cut, regulate temperature and a whole host of other activities, including reproduction.

Consider blood clotting. The body has a complex chemical circuitry to turn clotting on and off at precisely the right time. Clearly this is a complex software package with its material base in biology. But like any software and hardware, the software, the intelligence, had to precede the formation of hardware or the hardware would not know how to form itself to accept the software. One of the conundrums of the materialist theory of evolution is that if clotting took millions of years to evolve then everyone bled to death waiting for evolution to do its job.

It was always a marvel for me, growing up on a farm, to see animals give birth. Somehow they just knew how to do it, how to remove the amniotic sac, how to nurse, how to hear the cry of a specific baby over all the other cries, how to teach the baby what to fear and what was good, what to eat and what not to eat and so forth.

The farm animals did not know how to read books or hire experts yet they were capable of unlearned behavior that was directed and controlled by physiological drives and pure instinct. Together it formed a kind of biological software causing the animal to possess survival skills.

How do ants know how to build a mound or bees to build a hive? These are complex structures that have to withstand stressful forces. How does a bird know how to build a nest or migrate hundreds of miles to where it was born. How does a spider know how to spin an exotic web? Nature is full of wondrous examples of animals displaying complex unlearned behavior. When a baby horse is born a biological program turns on and the baby horse is walking within five minutes.

Animals can learn certain skills such as hunting and theses skills interface with unlearned behavior to create even greater marvels. Consider the cheetah running at 70 miles per hour and sweeping the hind legs from under a gazelle. Compare that to man made robots that can barley ascend a flight of stairs. Oh yes, the cheetah can reproduce, the robot cannot. Both the robot and the cheetah are controlled by complex software.

How does a beaver know how to build a dam? How does he know that the dam will result in a pond? How does the beaver know how to build a nest in the pond with underwater entrances? The beaver shows a special kind of intelligence. Dams and nests do not build themselves. These structures are very much a form of technology and the beaver is guided and motivated by an internal program, very much like a computer program. Who wrote the beaver program? Evolutionists attribute such complexities to the miracle of megaluck but such answers are flimsy and explain nothing. Other animals don't build dams to create ponds where special nests can be built with underwater entrances, just beavers. What a coincidence nature just happened to give this mammal special teeth to cut down trees so it can build a dam. And more, nature gave the beaver a special wide paddle type tail for strong swimming. When so few people can stay to task what makes the beaver such a disciplined and legendary worker? Unless the dam is completed and maintained it will not hold water to create a pond.

Evolutionists see no marvels here because to them everything is made of dead matter. Life, consciousness and intelligence are cosmic accidents.

What of hyper complexity and super miniaturization? The evolutionist does not want the audience to stop and ponder these attributes of nature because the evolutionist's whole world view unravels and self-destructs.

That so many people believe in evolution is no mystery. It is a function of governments programming their populations. It is garbage in and garbage out. The modern state does not want to recognize the existence of a higher authority in the universe. Philosophic materialism dispenses with God and then government is free to rule by brute force. Who will judge these men who own the power of the state? Will atoms condemn them? Will the elements revolt? Will the molecules and amino acids rise in protest? Will proteins resist? Who is there to judge the almighty state? Little wonder they place their faith in matter. Matter is their religion. It is their god and they love their god because he permits them to do anything.

Intelligence Is In The Software

When we start looking closer at biological programs our eyes are opened to an entirely non-materialistic way of seeing the universe. Consider photosynthesis.

Photosynthesis is the industrial process of a plant (all plants) that converts sunlight and carbon dioxide into carbohydrates (sugars) via the use of chlorophyll. This process is the highest of high technology. All the complex elements of this industrial process had to come into existence at the same time or no food would be produced. Obviously it had to come into existence in a small unit of time or no food. To infinitely complicate the matter the process had to be perfectly reproduced in each successive generation or no food.

What great luck, plants create food with the byproduct of oxygen that is a requirement of animal life and animal life produces carbon dioxide as the by-product of respiration that the plants need.

Photosynthesis is clearly a software program impressed into the tissues of the plant. Software, all software, is intelligence and has no physical existence. Software can't be seen. We can see the process of photosynthesis at work but we cannot see the intelligence that created or sustains it.

Consider the written words on this paper. Ink can be seen, a code of language may be surmised, but the words cannot be seen. More properly, words are concepts and concepts have no physical existence!

Do numbers have a physical existence? Of course not, and yet mankind's world is built on mathematics. Many things exist which have no physical existence. Imagine, non-physical existence!

Regarding the existence of hyper-complexity and super-miniaturization of photosynthesis, the materialists must offer tortured explanations hoping that gullibility will bridge the abyss. Could plants live millions of years without food while photosynthesis evolved in plants? If not, then the plants must have had a second way of obtaining and processing food. If so, why would dumb, blind nature go to all the trouble to evolve photosynthesis if the plant already had food?

Software Has No Physical Existence

Consider how an old fashioned phonograph works. A stylus, (a needle) sits in a grove while the record is mechanically turned. Imprinted on the walls of the grove are indentations. The stylus is made out of crystalline material that produces a small amount of electric current as the crystal moves back and forth. The electric current is amplified in several stages and ultimately converted to sound (mechanical energy). If music was encoded, the same music can be decoded and turned back into a replica of the original sound.

The software, the intelligence, is impressed into matter but it can't be seen. Only indentations may be seen (via a microscope) but the software has no physical existence.

Let's stand further back. The music was produced by the mind of a musician and transformed into sound by him playing his instrument. The recording device converted sound into an electric signal that causes a stylus to make indentations in the grove of the record. The reverse process decodes the information stored as indentations with conversion back to sound. The sound is decoded and interpreted by the mind of the listener. Thus, we went from one mind to another. Software is a creation of the mind. It begins and ends in the mind. All intelligence begins and ends in the mind. The mind? Every man-made object is an example of software. For example, a car is composed of different materials so it may hold passengers. The engine is shaped so that it may convert chemical energy into mechanical energy that turns the wheels. The software is impressed into the material parts, which when assembled, form a method of transportation. It all began in the inventor's mind.

The Mind

The mind? The materialist believes the human mind is produced by the brain. With both feet stuck in the mud of matter, what else could the materialist think? Does the brain produce the mind? Materialists everywhere have noted that every time they shoot a bullet into someone's head, the victim can't think anymore. Therefore, the mind is a product of the brain and only the brain. To a materialist the brain is a piece of meat that thinks. To a materialist everything reduces, always, to matter.

The brain! What a marvel of hyper-complexity and super-miniaturization. We're back to the same old problem of the materialist but this time it is even worse because the hyper-complexity and super-miniaturization is exponential.

Michael Denton is a world class microbiologist. His work is quite worthy. In "*Evolution: A Theory In Crisis*," Denton addresses the issue of the hyper-complexity of the human brain.

> In terms of complexity, an individual cell is nothing when compared with a system like the mammalian brain... Altogether the total number of connections in the human brain approaches 10^{15} or a thousand million million....

> Imagine an area about half the size of the USA (one million square miles) covered in a forest of trees containing ten thousand trees per square mile. If each tree contained one hundred thousand leaves, the total number of leaves in the forest would be 10^{15}, equivalent to the number of connections in the human brain!

The materialist theory is that this wonder was the result of evolutionary trial and error through the agency of mutation and natural selection. It appears that matter is capable of performing miracles.

The Complexity of the Brain

In *"Nature's Destiny,"* Denton dedicated an entire chapter to explain the DNA molecule. Regarding the super-miniaturization of DNA Denton states:

> The ability of DNA to store information is so efficient that all the information needed to specify an organism as complex as a man weighs less that a few trillionths of a gram. The information necessary to specify the design of all the organisms which have ever existed on the planet, a number, according to G.G. Simpson, of approximately 1 billion, could be easily compacted into an object the size of a grain of salt.

This is where the materialist dependence on megaluck kicks into overdrive. Imagine the software for a billion different organisms fitting into a space the size of a grain of salt? What a lucky break! Finally we come to the very essence of the materialist view of the origin of matter, life, consciousness and intelligence.

$$L = \text{Luck}$$
$$ML = \text{Megaluck}$$
$$O = \text{Origin}$$
$$L^{1,000,000,000,000,000,000,000} = ML$$
$$ML \rightarrow 0$$

The materialists claim that the human brain and the DNA molecule came into existence through a process of evolutionary trial and error. The mechanism of random mutation and natural selection produced the highest high-tech software in the universe. Hyper-gullibility is needed to bridge this abyss.

The human mind is the ultimate software. All the marvels of human technology existed first in the mind of a single individual person. The software precedes the hardware. The hardware doesn't know how to form on its own.

The Complexity Of The Cell

According to the materialist, life began in Darwin's pond where the first living cell came into existence. And quite a miracle it was. In "Nature's Destiny" Denton states:

> On any count the average cell must utilize close to a million unique adaptive structures and processes – more than the number in a jumbo jet. In this the cell seems to represent the ultimate expression in material form of compacted adaptive complexity – the complexity of a jumbo jet into a speck of dust invisible to the human eye.

What blinding megaluck, all the parts came together and what is more is that all the parts were perfectly compatible? Furthermore, all this megaluck had to be succeeded by more megaluck. The first cell had to reproduce perfectly in the first generation or life would abort.

The Mind of God

Please allow me to suggest another possibility. The first living creature did not come into existence via the agency of matter. It first existed in the mind of God. God's mind is the seat of all identity. Existence is basically epistemological not metaphysical. Before God created life, God created matter. Matter is informed by intelligence, by software, or it would not know how to behave. Like the groves of the record, matter holds the software. Is not matter ruthlessly regulated by universal and immutable laws? The laws of nature flow from the mind of God. Not only did God create the universe, His mind sustains its existence.

Existence? No one can define it. Science has no proof of existence. Great philosophers cannot deduce it. And yet man is certain he exists. No one can prove they are awake and yet they are certain they are awake.

Idealism's Axiom

So, we give you our unprovable starting point, our axiom; **God exists and from God's existence all existence flows**. Although the human brain has many marvels, the mind is not a product of the brain. The mind was created by God and God created a universal field the mind can access. It is from this universal field that the genius of man has its origin and is sustained. In this universal field we are connected to our Creator.

In the universal field we are connected to God's mind, the seat of all identity, the source of all knowledge.

The problem the materialist has with the brain based hypothesis of the mind is as follows:

Thousand of concepts are integrated to form generalizations. Many generations of generalizations are integrated to finally capture a great truth. Who would have every guessed E=MC²? How did Einstein surmise that it might be true? The chain of logic is so delicate, so extensive and so complex there are myriad ways to stumble into misapprehension. No brain could negotiate these shoals alone. Einstein directed his mind to the source of all identity and came back with an inkling of where to look.

The heresy of materialism is directing humanity to not consider the only true source of reality. Thus, humanity doesn't know how to behave and above all, humanity doesn't know how to find significance.

To idealists, the questions of value and significance are easy. We were created by God, for God's purpose. We have infinite value.

Allow me to let the materialist have the last word. The following are quotations from Bertrand Russell's *Mysticism and Logic* . This is the consummate poetic expression of philosophic materialism …

- That Man is the product of causes which had no prevision of the end they were achieving …
- That his origin, his growth, his hopes and fears, his loves and

his beliefs are but the outcome of accidental collocations of atoms ...

- That no fire, no heroism, no intensity of thought and feeling can preserve an individual life beyond the grave ...
- That all the labours of the ages, all the devotion, all the inspiration, all the noonday brightness of human genius are destined to extinction in the vast death of the solar system, and the whole temple of Man's achievement must inevitably be buried beneath the debris of a universe in ruins ...
- All these things, if not quite beyond dispute, are yet so nearly certain, that no philosophy which rejects them can hope to stand ...
- Only within the scaffolding of these truths, only on the firm foundation of unyielding despair, can the soul's habitation henceforth be safely built ...
- Brief and powerless is Man's life; on him and all his race the slow, sure doom falls pitiless and dark ....
- Blind to good and evil, reckless of destruction, omnipotent matter rolls on its relentless way; for Man, condemned today to lose his dearest, tomorrow himself to pass through the gate of darkness, it remains only to cherish, ere yet the blow falls, the lofty thoughts that ennoble his little day ... proudly defiant of the irresistible forces that tolerate, for a moment, his knowledge and his condemnation, to sustain alone, a weary but unyielding Atlas, the world that his own ideals have fashioned despite the trampling march of unconscious power.

Chapter 5

The Separation of
State and Philosophy

Let us assume for a moment that there really is God and from the existence of God all existence flows. This is "philosophic idealism." On the assumption that it is really true, then we live a specific kind of universe that is certainly not based on "matter." "Philosophic materialism" cannot be true. Metaphysics is the first branch of philosophy and it asks "what is the nature of the universe." **If God exists and existence flows from the existence of God then that information is the most important information any sentient being can have.**

If there is no God then the universe is a very different place. The materialists claim **in the beginning was matter and from matter alone comes the production of the universe**. The metaphysics of materialism is hostile to any idea of the existence of God. If there is God then it follows that the knowledge of God is the most important knowledge one could have. Consider how hostile the American establishment is to that knowledge. Government schools are not permitted to speak of the subject. The Supreme Court has banned cultural expressions of God and the media elite routinely ridicules philosophic idealism. **If there is God then the establishment is hostile to reality itself.**

The separation of church and state is, at its heart, a philosophic deception. The doctrine is actually the **separation of the state from philosophic idealism with an unstated commitment to materialism.** The shell game played by the Supreme Court is to assume that a religion is not a philosophy and because religion is a form of superstition it need not be considered philosophically.

The true doctrine of the current regime is "separation of state and philosophy." Consider how wrong the state is if God actually exists. Thus, the burning question is: **does God exist?**

The vast majority of Americans believe so. Only the government, the media and power elite are hostile to the idea of God, the recognition of God, cultural expressions regarding God and the knowledge of God. The system is anti-God.

The Charade

The charade the establishment plays is not to acknowledge its own philosophy, while attacking idealism. The argument is as follows: there are many different religions and the state must remain on neutral ground neither favoring one over another nor establishing a state sponsored religion. This they call "secularism."

The refutation of this phony argument is simple: there are many different philosophies and the state should not favor one over any other. Nor should the state create a state philosophy. In fact, the state should not bow to any philosophy. The state should be brainless and have no philosophy. This neutrality is secularism, the separation of state and philosophy.

The State Operates From a Hidden Philosophy

The problem is that the state does hold to specific philosophy and operates on a daily basis out of its philosophic view of reality. The truth is that all religions, whether they know it or not, are philosophies. They all have a theory of metaphysics, epistemology, ethics and esthetics. Any godless philosophy has the same. Religions are philosophies. Indeed there are many idealistic philosophies and many materialistic philosophies. Unfortunately, reality is complex and if the members of the Supreme Court are not up to the challenge they should resign instead of dismissing idealism. On the assumption that God exists and from God's existence all existence flows, then it follows that idealism is reality and that materialism is a fraud.

On the assumption that God exists and from God's existence all existence flows, then everything changes. (Parenthetically, I would like to say that everyone thinks they know what "existence" is. However, no one can define existence, not science and certainly not the Supreme Courts. All systems of knowledge have an unprovable starting point, a set of axioms). The Supreme Court has never identified its means to knowledge. It has never identified its philosophy let alone the axioms of its philosophy.

Choose Life

Unfortunately the Supreme Court has kicked God out of society, inviting all the attendant consequences. If there is God I should think that it is not profitable to offend God. Ethically speaking, everything changes the minute one accepts God as the axiomatic fact. If God created man then He created man with a specific nature which means that a specific course of action is needed for man to exist. This specific course of action is called God's law. All actions add to life or subtracts from life. Therefore all actions are moral in nature. The standard of value is the life of man. The good gives life and the evil is anti-life. On the assumption that there is God then it behooves man to discover the moral law, the law of God. Anything less involves the negation of life.

Please note that I have stated my axiom: God exists. The corollary axiom is: from God's existence all existence flows. This is the unprovable starting point of idealistic knowledge. It is the axiom of western civilization and certainly the axiom of the constitutional republic founded in the United States of America. The rest is a long chain of logic, rigorous in nature but then again any system of philosophy is equally rigorous and many will come to disagreement over specifics.

Phony Secularism

Consider the materialistic axiom of the Supreme Court: matter exists and from matter, alone, comes the production of the universe. How does conscious, intelligent life come into existence? It is the law of the land that public schools cannot acknowledge the idealist position that God created the universe, life and man. Only evolution may be taught. This is tantamount to court ordered censorship. The phony secularism of the Court is a godless religion. It exists as a state sponsored monopoly, the very thing forbidden in the First Amendment of the Constitution of the United States.

The Supreme Court claims that its impossible view of the origin of the universe, life, consciousness and intelligence, is scientific. They believe in evolution and they will not permit philosophic idealism to have expression in the public square. This is not a neutral position, especially when the vast majority of Americans believe in the existence of God. The secularism of the establishment is a con game. Although their system claims to uphold tolerance it is completely intolerant of philosophic idealism. There is no place at the table for philosophic idealism nor will there ever be. Philosophic materialism, posing as secularism, is eternally hostile to philosophic idealism. There is an eternal contradiction between materialism and idealism. There is an eternal war and as materialism grows in power it will seek the annihilation of its enemy. On the assumption that God exists the con game is easy to see for what it is.

The assumption of the Supreme Court is either that God does not exist or that God is irrelevant. Matter reigns. This, of course, is the worst kind of slander against God. On the assumption there is God, it is fool hearty to make material misrepresentations

49

against God. Drunken with its power, the Supreme Court invites disaster. The members of the Supreme Court operate from the assumption they will not be required to appear in God's Court to account for their felonies.

Libido Dominandi

The members of the Supreme Court do not believe in God and therefore they do not think there will come a day of judgment. They are materialists and matter has no power to judge them. They think that because God does not exist, that man is a kind of god and that the state, the collective, is the only reality, the standard of value, the alpha and omega.

The appeal of materialism is that it gives license to mix a cocktail of lusts and drink your brains out. For those who love *libido dominandi* (the lust of domination) statism is quite intoxicating. What is the biggest game in town ------ the imperial welfare/ warfare state!

Materialist Ethics

Reflective people understand that something is terribly wrong with our society. Consider the problem of ethics under materialism. To live we must act but how shall we act? How does materialism inform us? Materialism offers us a short life followed by eternal death. However, eternal death is absurd and it makes life itself absurd. Materialists usually cobble together an ethical view, borrowing heavily from idealism. Materialism often borrows from

Christ, embracing the golden rule. The materialist understands the chaos of the war of "all against all." So they offer a truce: I will recognize your right to life if you recognize mine. However betrayal abounds and truces are made to be broken.

Our first question is where does the concept "rights" come from? Did the Supreme Court create life? How then can it issue rights? The founders of the United States believed that God created life and a man's right to life comes from God.

Rights? Under materialism "rights" are merely "prerogatives." The state may infringe upon your life, liberty and property per its *libido dominandi*. The equation yields to the recognition of each other's "state-given prerogatives." Rights are not rights any longer. They are merely temporary, mutable, arbitrary options. The state can and does infringe upon the life, liberty and property of its citizens. If the state can prey upon its subjects, then why can't one man prey upon another? If matter cannot punish there is nothing to fear except the retribution of other men. It is all a matter of can you get away with it?

The Contradiction In Materialist Ethics

The rules are arbitrary, contradictory and self serving to those who have captured power. Who could possibly admire such rules or the mere mortals who create them? Why can't a man make up his own rules? Why have any rules at all? What is important about another person's life? So he loves his life. What's important about that? Why exactly shouldn't one man prey upon another?

Why shouldn't one man fulfill his passions at the expense of another? We are all going to die anyway and that absurdity means that everything is absurd. The very concept of justice is absurd. There is nothing important about life. If a man thinks his life is important that is merely his opinion and if my opinion is that his life is unimportant, how will we resolve the difference of opinion but by fists and guns? The materialists understand the practical need for common rules for society to live by, but materialism itself is a contradiction of any system of ethics. Per Dostoyevsky: if there is no God then all things are permissible.

This is how the materialist wolves play the game. There is nothing they would not permit themselves. Their only inhibition is to avoid the retribution of others. Thus, the wolves pose as the benefactors of humanity.

Violence In The Land

Pascal said that if men who believe in God are as wicked as they are, how will men behave when they don't believe in God? We got the answer. The 20th century belonged to the materialist wolves. It was a century of war and mass murders, of genocide and every form of wickedness. The 20th century was the Mount Everest of human depravity. With a metaphysics that denies reality and an epistemology that denies identity is it any wonder that there is violence in the land? The ultimate problem of materialism is that it has no moral law.

The Separation Of The Church And Its Head

The Supreme Court plays its game without ever having identified its axioms. It has not identified its materialistic metaphysics nor has it identified its theory of knowledge and certainly not the basis of it ethics. The Supreme Court practices separation of state and philosophy claiming that philosophical idealism is not a philosophy but merely a superstition, not worthy of public debate. The Court routinely smuggles in its philosophic materialism in the name of secularism. It's a con game. **The separation of church and state is really the separation of the church and its head.** The constitution of the United States forbids the government from establishing a state religion, like materialism. And it also forbids Congress from making any law prohibiting the "free exercise" of religion. What to do? Ditch the constitution? Play the con game of secularism and mix your cocktail of lust and drink your brains out.

The Banishment Of God

When ninety (plus) percent of the American people believe in God, the Supreme Court is not about to become confessional about its philosophic materialism and more specifically about its atheism. What amazes me is how few people, especially Christians, understand the atheistic malice behind the court's persecution of philosophic idealism. Let us pull off the fig leaf. The entire establishment is anti-God and anti-Christ. The feigned neutrality of their secularism is merely a mechanism for banishing God from society.

The Abortion Holocaust

Consider an illustration how they play the game with respect to abortion. The Supreme Court looked into the 14th Amendment and behold it found a "right to privacy." It then usurped the power of Congress, it usurped the rights of the States, and via judicial edict, made abortion legal. Abortion was a matter of "privacy." Forty five million abortion deaths later, the slaughter is competing for first place in the history of genocides. What is remarkable is that the materialists do not think a thing of it. Nor do they think a thing of having embraced terrible contradictions to have their will in society. Nor do they think a thing of having trashed the constitution and the rule of law.

The Materialist Wolves

There is not anything a materialist will not do. It is only a matter of being able to fully realize the implications of their own philosophy. However, a house divided against itself cannot endure. There is no honor among wolves. These wolves will join in a pack when they think it is to their advantage but they will betray their brothers when their calculus indicates a different conclusion.

When society makes a hero of the wolf, the wolves abound. Why die for your country when it can die for you? Why be faithful to your wife when what she does not know will not hurt her? Why not cheat in business when cheating can be so profitable? Why shouldn't the strong exploit the weak? That is survival of the fittest. Why not deceive your friends when life is only a pretense anyway? Family? Family is just a four letter word. War, to the victor goes the spoils. Politics, just another kind of war. Bribery and blackmail? Business as usual.

The spirit of the age filters down and the exploited transforms into exploiters. The average person hears the clarion call of the materialist ethic. The "golden rule" is for suckers they think. The streets become dangerous, your home is no longer safe. It is "the war of all against all." What good is your money if you have to live in a state of fear?

Under the current interpretation of the doctrine of the separation of church and state, the state claims that the church may not have cultural expression on government property. However, considering the comprehensive scope and size of mega-government, the encroachment is almost total. When ubiquitous government stands everywhere, where then can the church stand?

A Semantic Clue

A parting thought; There is a semantic give away that provides a strong hint to the true nature of the founding. Please note that we do not have separation of *mosque* and state, *synagogue* and state or *churches* and state. We have separation of church and state. Which church, the Christian church? The United States was founded by philosophic idealists specifically Christian idealists. Originally, secularism was an agreement to not engage in denominational doctrinal disputes in a public setting. Nor were the framers of the constitution deist. They were Christian, and what they had in common was Christian Idealism.

Materialism Will Destroy All It Touches

Today the doctrine of separation has come to mean the opposite. The first amendment clearly protects the church from the state and yet the reading today is that the state needs protection from the church. This inversion was necessary for materialism to supplant idealism.

The materialists have won, but the victory is only temporary. The materialists will destroy the culture, the currency and the economy. The pain will provoke deep thought and revive what can never be killed – reality – philosophic idealism.

This is the trajectory of philosophical materialism, from premise to conclusion. It is forced play. The premise contains the conclusion. Materialism will destroy all it touches.

The Ultimate Software

Consider a marble statue like Michelangelo's *David*. It is clear to see that the statue has a material base but it is primarily software with the artist making an esthetic statement. In other words, the statue has a materialistic aspect that is insignificant compared to the idealistic aspect. Such is the nature of art.

Likewise, matter itself is composed of two aspects, hardware and software. The Supreme Court cannot see the software impressed in hardware – the Intelligence. Thus, it denies the existence of the Artist.

Chapter 6
Matter Is the Creator?

It took many centuries for mankind to come to an understanding of the nature of matter. The ancient Greeks used to endlessly debate the nature of the real world; some combination of earth, wind, fire, water or other elements. The Greeks (and Romans) believed in a pantheon of capricious gods who were responsible for the good and bad fortunes of men. Both cultures were stillborn, unable to advance to the periodic chart. That task was achieved by only Christian Europe. Science was the study of God's creation; thinking God's thoughts after God had thought them. These Christians were philosophic idealists and they brought the world the scientific revolution that lead to the industrial revolution. Steeped in revised history the present generation has no appreciation for what Christian idealism accomplished. The industrial revolution could have never happened without centuries of advancement in social and political institutions; constitutional government upholding the rights of man; rule of law, the private ownership of property, contractual law enforced by a court system, patent law, copyright of intellectual property and more.

Neither the Greeks nor Romans nor any other ancient and pagan civilization, were able to abolish slavery or to step beyond their view of a reality dominated by capricious gods. The scientific and industrial revolutions only happened in the Christian west. Materialist historians cannot possibly understand why.

Nor was belief in a single god an automatic guarantor of progress. Islam postulates an infinite but arbitrary power that could declare vice to be virtue and virtue to be vice. Why is the universe the way it is? Because of the sovereign whim of Allah. A sovereign whim does not lead to science nor civilized institutions.

Who can doubt the power of modern science and engineering? The marvels of technology are everywhere for everyone to see. With these marvels have come great wealth and power and ease of living. Modern science led to the industrial revolution and to the explosion of knowledge.

Mankind has come a long way in understanding the nature of matter and the forces that regulate it. Who could possibly deny the monumental achievements of science and engineering? Matter will obey anyone who holds the keys to its knowledge. It is this knowledge that is the basis for agreement among men as to the nature of knowledge itself - epistemology. This is the universal common ground upon which people may agree.

The Cult Of Materialism Goes Too Far

But then they go too far. A truth that loses its proportion becomes just another grotesque lie. In physics class they will tell you that science never asks "why" because it does not know "why" - it only asks "how." Yet the cult of materialism goes far beyond the domain of science and in the name of science it declares the impossible to be true. From whence did we come? The materialists boldly trumpet that matter possesses a magical ability to transform itself into more complex forms until at last, with big doses of time and lots of megaluck, man appears. With regard to origin, science neither knows "why" nor "how." Never-the-less the materialists boldly assert that they know. To carry their arguments they resort to ad hominem; only unenlightened fools would disagree with them. Because they have captured the taxing authority they use the federal treasury to finance endless media programming about their theory. Like the ocean pounding the shore the establishment pounds the public with its materialistic creation myth.

Another Abyss

Although we know a great deal more about matter than the ancient Greeks, my suspicion is that there is more knowledge ahead of us than behind. The materialists stand between the abyss of the infinitely large and the abyss of the infinitely small declaring that they know it all. My guess is that there is another abyss, the abyss of materialist delusion. It appears there is more to the universe than just matter.

Big Science Contradicts Itself

From whence did matter come? In the 20th century there were two dominant and contradictory theories. The Steady State Theory said the universe had no beginning and that there is an infinite egress of cause and effect. The Big Bang Theory said that the universe began some fifteen and a half billion years ago. What was before the Big Bang? Theories abound but no one really knows. The cosmologists sound increasingly like theologians – the universe "came from nothing," they say. Hundreds of years ago theologians said that God created the universe "from nothing." Decades ago there was a great materialistic clamor for the Steady State Theory. That big science contradicts itself seems not to bother anyone.

Departing From Gradualism

We have come a long way since science conceived of the atom as a miniature solar system with electrons orbiting about a nucleus sun. Science has identified over 60 subatomic particles. In my undergraduate years they taught us that matter requires vast amounts of time to evolve into living creatures. The doctrine of "gradualism" was the only excepted possibility. "Quantum Leap," was strictly forbidden. This theory claimed that evolution could be explained by dramatic mass mutations causing huge evolutional leaps. Decades later Stephen Jay Gould, a leading evolutionist, came to espouse quantum leaps (Punctuated Equilibrium). Such leaps are akin to miracles which was why the old school held furiously to gradualism. If nature moved in quantum leaps, who was to say that God had not intervened in nature? Materialists hate such a thought. Gould too, as a marxist and atheist, would object.

Matter, to Gould was capable of producing its own miracles. A bird could lay an egg and out could come a mammal. How? Somehow? No science required.

Reversion To The Mean

Darwin's theory of natural selection was an attempt to give evolution a mechanism that makes it work to produce new species or even life itself. We have shown in Chapter 2 that natural selection cannot and does not work (macroevolution). But there is another problem for the cult of materialism. Evolving matter is a tall claim. Certainly there must be some universal force, like gravity, that makes evolution work. There must be some law like the "Law of Increasing Order." However, there is no such law. Indeed, the second law of thermodynamics is the opposite: the law of increasing disorder – **the law of entropy**.

If matter moves against the gradient of increasing disorder, then it should be easy enough to scientifically identify. Alas, no such law exists. As I said before, matter will obey any master but it does so within its own nature. To be the master of matter, the master must obey the laws of matter. One of the laws is "reversion to the mean." The theory of evolution of matter depends heavily on massive luck through eons of time. Such an idea however, flies in the face of reality. Reversion to the mean says that it's impossible to string together enough lucky accidents to create the hyper-complexity witnessed in the simplest of life forms.

Matter Is The Creator

Every casino in the world understands the ruthless nature of the law of averages. Science does too, in half of its schizophrenic soul, the half that understands "probabilities." When it comes to evolution, science suddenly gets emotional. **When Big Science is in bed with Big Government, Big Science must do the will of Big Government.** Big Science says what it is required to say. The quid pro quo is easy to see, for anyone who cares to see. No one likes to think that he is an intellectual prostitute. Like everyone else scientists are quite capable of self-deceit. The cocktail of lusts is different for a state funded scientist than it is for others. There is more emphasis on intellectual pride, position, rank and status. It can be quite intoxicating. Belief in evolution is expected. To not believe is to destroy your career. "In the beginning there was matter and matter, alone. The production of the universe comes from matter. **Matter is the creator**."

Blaise Pascal

It was Blaise Pascal, the French mathematician and inventor of the computer, who pointed out the implication of believing or not believing in God. If there is no God, he argued, then we will all end up in eternal death with nothing to account for and no one to account to. However, if the universe is structured differently and if there is a Creator, then there may be a deep downside risk in denying God and His rule. It is all a gigantic wager with infinite risk on one side of the wager.

The great appeal of materialism is that there is no one to account to and nothing to account for. Materialism boldly pushes all its chips in the middle, wagering everything in a state of defiance.

The Idea Of Power

Big Government has many big friends; Big Science, Big Media, Big Military, Big IRS, Big Foundations, Big Business, Big Welfare, Big Warfare, Big Hollywood, Big Education, Big Judiciary, Big Congress, Big Senate and the Big Supreme Court. The idea of God gets in the way of the idea of power.

Unearned power is intoxicating. It is corrupting. It leads to delusion and destruction. The materialists believe that they are safe because matter cannot punish them. They look upon average men and say to themselves "We dominate these men for their own good." They say, "Because these men are stupid, it is our right to rule them." They say "It is all part of the struggle for existence and the survival of the fittest."

Chapter 7
The Materialist War On The Family

To paraphrase conservative columnist, Joseph Sobran, there are three institutions of society hated by a tyrannical state: private property because it allows independence from the state, the church because it is a competing authority and the family because it is a competing loyalty. In this chapter we will explore the materialism's war on the family.

Traditional Marriage

Defined traditional marriage is a monogamous moral and legal relationship, a special union achievable between a man and a woman to advance their love and to create a home where children may be born and cared for. The family creates and prepares the next generation so that our kind may continue its existence. The love between a husband and wife is much more than just an erotic relationship. The ancient script said it best, "and they being two shall become one flesh." The ancient vow was "'til death do us part." The ancient order commanded a "husband to love his wife as Christ loved the church."

The love and loyalty between husbands and wives and between parents and children were believed to be ordained by God. Above all, the family was united by its loyalty to God and to God's moral order.

Laws To Protect Marriage And The Family

Society constructed a comprehensive matrix of laws to protect the marriage and the family, including laws to prohibit adultery, cohabitation, prostitution, abortion, bigamy, polygamy, pornography and homosexuality. There were laws to prevent rough men from using vulgar and profane language in mixed company. There were statutory rape laws to protect girls before the "age of consent." Marriage was considered the standard of value. What was good for marriage was valuable and good for society; what was bad for marriage was bad for society. Society recognized that sexuality needs to be constrained and that the libertine leads to chaos. Society had decorum and dignity.

Deconstruction Of The Family

Let us consider the materialists view of marriage and the family. It has long been the goal of various kinds of socialism (the dominant political form of materialism) to abolish or deconstruct the family. Marxian socialists openly call for the abolition of the family. The communist manifesto is quite clear. American socialists have preferred a gradual deconstruction. Let us consider the dismantling of the protective law outlined above.

Adultery

It is amazing to consider the utter collapse of sexual standards within my own life time. One of the metrics of a sane civilization is how it controls sexuality, not how it embraces the libertine. In America today there is ubiquitous smut on every channel. Society is constantly bombarded with obscenity. Every day the materialist sewer pours out a new torrent of toxicity. The number one industry of the internet is hardcore pornography. The environment is saturated with cheap sex. It is not possible for grandparents to watch television with their grandchildren without being ambushed by sexual filth. In public schools they teach twelve year old girls how to get started and how to get abortions when birth control backfires.

To a materialist, sex is about gratification. Women are masturbation machines. Of course, there is no better way to destroy a marriage than by adultery. Materialism advocates open marriage and clandestine extra-marital affairs. The entertainment media routinely glamorizes adultery. Prior to the 1960s marriage was a lifelong contract and required legal justification for termination. Adultery constituted grounds for divorce. There were civil laws against adultery; if people were adulterous they hid it, as they should.

Cohabitation

Cohabitation is living together in a sexual relationship without the commitment of marriage itself. Before the sexual revolution, cohabitation was prohibited by law and in many states such laws are still effective, although not enforced. The reason why our ancestors made cohabitation illegal was because it is a contradiction to marriage. It is an attempt to have some of the benefits of marriage without embracing the responsibility. At any time one may cut and run so cohabitators make their love with one eye on the exit sign.

Although some cohabitators eventually marry, many have entered the estate with a partner who is nothing more than a practical compromise. Almost always one of the partners is operating on a false set of expectations, strung along with the possibility of marriage and family.

Cohabitation is basically a dishonest relationship and our ancestors understood that. That is why they defended marriage.

Materialist society has difficulty giving a name to a cohabitator. He is more than a boyfriend but much less than a husband. Some trendy psychologist came up with the term "significant other," and it stuck. The truth is that there is a much better term; **"insignificant other."**

Prostitution

Liberal materialists often argue that prostitution is a victimless crime. Only a jaded barbarian would dare to make such a callused argument. Prostitution is the savage sexual exploitation of young women by pimps and johns who ply them with drugs and seduce them with money. To a materialist there is no form of consenting sex that would represent true perversion. The only moral criterion for materialist sex is "consent." If there is consent then any kind of sex is permissible. (However, there are unspoken exceptions; for the elite, consent is not an obstacle to their lust.) Prostitutes serve the perverse appetites of deeply troubled men. In a sense men are victims too. The whole institution is so utterly sordid and so intensely neurotic that any sane society would make it illegal and keep it that way. The State of Nevada has legalized prostitution so the state government may profit from the trade. That makes the state legislature nothing more than a gang of materialist pimps trafficking in human misery.

Prostitution is a contradiction to marriage and society is well served to keep it illegal. Materialists often argue that society should not legislate morality. A more intensely stupid argument has never been made. The law that prohibits murder is a moral law. The law that prohibits drunk driving is a moral law. Any law that prohibits any human action is preserving some assumed moral order. A sane society has the right and responsibility to protect itself and its members with laws that legislate morality. That is what law and order is all about.

Abortion

Prior to Roe v. Wade in 1972, abortion was illegal in every state. The United States Supreme Court usurped the federal legislature and fifty state governments making abortion legal via judicial fiat. There have been 45 million abortions since that decision.

The materialists got their ultimate formula for the public promotion of promiscuous sex. Birth control backed up by the abortion table, opened up the legs of millions of American women. Many of them came to regret their actions.

Our Christian ancestors understood the issues quite well. Something dies in an abortion. That something is human. What else could it possibly be? The very reason it needs to be killed is because it is human and if it is not killed, it will become an unwanted responsibility. The materialist Supreme Court is responsible for the greatest mass murder in world history.

Many young women have been seduced by materialists into engaging in promiscuous sex with the idea that there would not be physical and psychological consequences.

Older materialists know that abortion is a sort of baptism into materialism. As a woman ages how does she morally justify her action? She cannot and so she defends abortion while harboring contradictions that can never be reconciled.

Young men and women do not understand the issues that surround abortion. They have been deceived by sophisticated materialist wolves who hate God and God's moral law. The ancient text is very clear: the shedding of innocent blood is an abomination to God. Materialists believe only in matter and matter has no power to judge them.

Bigamy and Polygamy

What is so morally special about monogamy? Why exactly shouldn't a man have two or more wives? Why shouldn't one of those wives be a man? The materialists have such low standards they cannot think of a reason to resist their temptations.

The answer is simple, one woman can give a man what all the women in the world cannot give, her love and intimacy. A man can get sex from a harem but not the love of one wife. Our ancestors knew what we have lost, that God made the woman the complement of the man and they being two shall become one flesh. In a very real sense a married couple is a single entity. What materialist barbarian could possibly understand that? And so it was that society traditionally has not allowed marriage of multiple parties.

It is ironic that materialistic feminism has advanced the libertine to the point that monogamy is under siege. When monogamy falls, men will want multiple wives as they once had and the old curse of polygamy will have been recreated. Feminism will have helped to recreate the worst form of male chauvinism possible.

Pornography

It used to be illegal and still should be. Pornography is the media display of nudity with the motivation to elicit a sexual response from the audience. Hardcore pornography is the media display of prostitutes involved in sexual acts with the motivation to elicit a sexual response from the audience.

Pornographers portray every form of human perversion and such perversions call especially to the young and impressionable. The whole purpose of pornography is to provoke a sexual response. Pornographic orgasm can become a narcotic. The young imprint on various perversions. The sexual criminal, Ted Bundy reported that is was pornography that set him on the road as a serial rape murderer. Where in pornography do we see anything that is spiritual or human?

Sex on the left end of the bell curve has no conception of sex on the right end of the bell curve. Perverse sex is a narcotic and violence is an amplifier. Since the Supreme Court made the world safe for pornography the pornographers have marketed every form of depravity imaginable. It festers in the human soul. It's degrading to women and to humanity itself. Once the court got on this the slippery slope it has been all downhill. We have become a pornographic society; we think pornographically. We speak pornographically.

Our Christian ancestors understood that pornography was a misuse of human sexuality and a contradiction to marriage. To think that the spiritual inheritance of Americans has been squandered on cheap and profane sexual perversions is beyond comprehension. As rock star, Madonna says, "I'm a material girl in a material world."

Homosexuality

Our ancestors understood what was in the closet and made protective laws to keep it in the closet. Our ancestors understood that there would be hell to pay if it came out. Heterosexual decadence was the guarantor that homosexual decadence would be socially accepted. One kind of decadence must tolerate another; and so it is that America now has its first political sex movement pressuring politicians for ever more liberalization including marriage and adoption. Homosexuality is a contradiction of marriage. When a man has sex with a man he is having sex in another man's sewer. **<u>Sewer sex is not the moral equivalent of procreative sex</u>**. Our ancestors understood that perfectly well.

Homosexuals are not content to be tolerated by society. They demand moral approval. They demand moral applauds. They have successfully lobbied to have the government commence a campaign to "normalize" homosexuality without a vote from the people. Homosexuals now demand the legislation of "hate crimes" and "hate speech." This book along with the Holy Bible and millions of other books will be burned in the night if homosexuals have their way. Heil to the Beast!

Above all, homosexuals are demanding that government legalize homosexual marriage, a contradiction in terms. No baby ever came out of the rectum of a man. **Every baby has a right to a mother.** The country has spoken in many referendums, but the Imperial Judiciary presses the issue in favor of homosexuals.

Legalization has lead to normalization and even now in government elementary schools children are taught the wonders of sodomy. Need I say more? An excellent book to read is *Homosexuality: A Freedom Too Far* by Charles W. Socarides.

No Fault Divorce

The first major mutation of marriage was to create "divorce upon demand." In the 1960s, "no-fault divorce" was born and with it came an epidemic of divorce. No-fault divorce meant that if your spouse petitioned for divorce you were committed to an irresistible legal process. Who would get the kids and the marital home? Who would pay child support? What would the rules be for a post-divorce relationship? Whose standards would apply? The state would decide all this and much more.

By promoting mass divorce the state had interjected itself into the heart of the family, micromanaging every aspect of human life. When politicians proclaim that they do not want the government in the bedroom I cannot imagine what they mean. For decades the government has been deeply involved in the bedroom and every other room.

With the contractual element taken out of marriage the state removed any moral obligation to conduct oneself according to a code of ethics. In a contract both parties agree to certain terms. No-fault divorce abrogated the contractual element in marriage leaving marriage itself without definition. The person petitioning for divorce was given power to invite the state into the private life of the defendant, even though the defendant had done nothing illegal and nothing to provoke a divorce. The courts could assume authority over the children who automatically become wards of the court at the time of the petition for divorce. No-fault divorce gave totalitarian control of divorcing and divorced families to the government. The government always seeks novel ways to expand its authority and no-fault divorce was a real brainstorm. No-fault divorce, destroyed Christian marriage and in its place was born materialistic marriage. Consider the utter chaos that has followed.

Concomitant to the rise of materialistic marriage and divorce was the rise of the modern socialist welfare state. Its primary client was and is the female. With few exceptions, only women could obtain welfare. Welfare worked wonderfully to promote divorce. Mom had someone else to pay the bills so why not boot the ol' man out?

Universal Female Custody Upon Demand

The second major mutation of marriage is what I call "universal female custody upon demand." In any adjudicated case, except for female default, women are always awarded custody. The marital home is part of the package. Child support follows. **Dad is systematically turned into a visitor, a big, dumb, powerless, neutered, fairy that the kids hustle for bucks.**

It is hardly a surprise that divorced families became an engine of criminality and pathology. With government financing the welfare state it was inevitable that divorce would become big business. What a bonanza for attorneys, judges, social workers, psychologists, police, abuse workers, sex abuse workers, court workers and others.

The government found a willing ally in feminism. The government provides a few billion dollars of annual subsidy to the feminist movement. I call it Aid to Dependent Feminists. Gender equity would be brought into grade school. The diversity police would be stationed in every college classroom waiting for an intellectual enemy to violate politically correct speech. Although many feminists are little more than common sluts, they feign Victorian prudishness when it comes to sexual harassment standards. Corporations would be brought into gender equity submission. Diversity? There is no diversity in America. We have an intellectual monoculture. The product of state education is a dreadful uniformity that produces standardized dummy-downs that will be subservient to their masters. There is nothing diverse about diversity and nothing tolerant about tolerance.

The Abuse Industry

Even more Orwellian is the rise of the abuse industry. Without due process of law, a father could be evicted from his home by a mere accusation by his wife. Even with no marks, no sprains, no broken bones, no fat lip, no evidence at all, the accusation is good enough to have dad arrested and evicted.

For the mere accusation of sexual abuse dad could be evicted and denied any access to his children. Here he faces criminal prosecution. Many innocent men have faced the horror of a system gone mad. **A man's home is his wife's castle.**

What of visitation? The system is fully aware that children make wonderful weapons and that denial of visitation is widespread and common place. The truth is that it would be easy to enforce by letting Her Highness spend a weekend in jail. Alas, the system prefers to let her be as belligerent as she pleases. Dad has to endlessly retain an attorney to plead for visitation. The court orders it again and Her Highness disregards the order with impunity. The benefactors of the welfare state are very creative at inventing strategies to, as scholar Stephen Baskerville says, **"mine the pockets of middle class men."** It is all about money and power.

No-fault divorce and universal female custody upon demand were the two mutations of traditional marriage that destroyed marriage. Consider the tsunami of divorce, of broken homes and broken hearts. These broken homes are an engine of pathology destroying America.

No-fault divorce and universal female custody upon demand succeeded because it destroyed the balance of power in the family creating an incentive to divorce and spawned a whole set of discriminatory laws against fathers. We shall close with a list outlining some of these laws and policies. How do you kill a family? Cut off its head.

The balance of power between male and female, father and mother, has been systematically destroyed in favor of female dominance at law. The following is a list of female advantages over male.

Laws Used To Create Wars Between The Genders

1. A married woman may legally abort her child without her husband's permission. This underscores the materialistic view that the male is merely a sperm donor and that the child is not a person.
2. Although a wife may abort without permission from her husband, he cannot compel an abortion, even if the child is not his.
3. A husband is legally and financially responsible for any child born to the marriage even though it is not his.
4. Except for rich men and in cases of female default (for example, prison, abandonment, hospitalization or death) women universally receive custody of children and all that comes with it, the marital home, child support and executive power over the children.
5. Denial of court ordered visitation is common place and not punished.
6. Alienation, turning the kids against their father, is commonplace and tolerated by the courts.
7. Any woman can tell any amount of lies in family court and not fear prosecution for perjury.
8. Fathers routinely have their children taken from them by judges. In most, if not all states, men are not allowed to have jury trials. Juries would never do to families what judges do. Federal policy is executed via the judiciary.

9. Women frequently scam the welfare system. When they are caught they are not prosecuted or even made to pay back the money. Often the ex-husband has to pay it back.

10. Women are the primary clients of the welfare state, not men.

11. When an unmarried woman misrepresents her fecundity to a man, he is still financially liable for her unilateral decision to become pregnant.

12. If an unmarried woman becomes pregnant she may abort over the objection of the man. If she decided to keep the child he cannot compel an abortion and must be liable for child support.

13. Paternal grandparents have no rights of visitation with their son's children.

14. Any woman may call the police and allege physical abuse. Even without any physical evidence the male will be arrested, booked and placed into the system for prosecution. He must prove his innocence. He will be evicted from his home without due process of law and may have a personal protection order filed against him.

15. Any woman may allege sexual abuse of one of her children and 800 years of constitutional protections are thrown out the window. Without due process of law, the man will be evicted from his home, arrested, booked, released on bail and prosecuted. He will have to pay child support. The allegation of sex abuse may be used in family court to obtain permanent custody. He will have to pay tens of thousand of dollars for an attorney and all this while he is trying to fund a new residence and hold down a job. The custodial mother can smear his name in public with impunity and even try to destroy his employment and all without fear of correction from the court. The woman does not have to retain an attorney to prosecute the sex abuse case; the state does this for her. If subsequently it is discovered that she lied the

system will not prosecute her. The man will get his day in court after a year or two. By then his children have been taken from him and his property has been transferred to his accuser.

16. After divorce there are often many conflicts that have to be resolved by the court. The custodial mother does not have to hire an attorney, the court ancillary will represent her interest against the non-custodial father.

17. The system is quick to increase child support and even base it on overtime and/or second jobs. However, if a man loses overtime or his second job (or his primary job) he quickly falls into "arrears." The courts will not make timely adjustments even if loss of income is not his fault.

18. Draconian measures for collection of child support have been federally mandated. These include seizure of assets, seizure of professional licenses and up to four years in prison. Arrearages compound at exorbitant interest rates. (See Title 42/Chapter 7/ Subchapter IV/Part D/Subsection **666**)

19. Child support accrues for men in prison with above market interest rates. Such men become "debt slaves" to the state.

20. Men are traumatized by divorce and loss of their children but the courts are unsympathetic. The court will not adjust child support accordingly.

Conclusion

Kinsey: Crimes and Consequences by Judith A. Reisman, chronicles the early assault of materialists to deconstruct marriage by attacking the laws that protected marriage and families.)

Materialism is toxic. It poisons everything it touches. It forever roams in the labyrinth of its own creation, a philosophical dead end that gives it permission to pursue any lust but to never find satisfaction in its expression. Materialism forecloses its options; the universe is material. The spiritual is an illusion. Doomed to extinction, each materialist holds unyielding despair. Life is meaningless. It rampages by and then your days are gone. "What was it all for?" asked Ayn Rand at the end of her life, speaking for the entire cult of matter.

Materialism destroys everything it touches. It corrupts the people. It has squandered the legacy of our ancestors. It has pushed a once great nation into insolvency and it has debauched the currency. An event is coming where the equation will be rebalanced. America is about to be corrected by reality. The full measure of human suffering will be on an unimaginable scale, and as the drama and spectacle of human suffering unfolds consider that America has forsaken its heritage in favor of materialism.

Chapter 8
Does God Believe In You?

The real question is "does God believe in you?" Life is over in a flash. They throw dirt in your face and call it a day. Everyone obsesses about being remembered but that's the one thing that is a certainty. You will be forgotten, and sooner than you think. A moment of impatient silence and they're off to the materialist race again. Death, the great equalizer. In the grave the richest man in the world and the poorest has the same net worth. The powerful are helpless to halt its advance. The mighty fall to its final blow.

Death renders life an absurdity. What was life all about? What was it all for, the struggle to achieve values? So you held them for a moment in time and now you must lay them down. Without life, you can hold nothing. All you cherished, all that you ever loved must be surrendered to the absurdity of death.

What was it that you lived for? No matter how deeply you drank of the cup of pleasure the thirst could not be quenched. Now that you face eternal darkness, pleasure is all the more illusive. Was it pleasure that you lived for?

It will not be long now and you will face the final moment. As you pass through the portal of death, you will meet eternal demise or you will meet the next manifestation of life.

If you recall, at different moments of your life, you trashed humanity for its hypocrisy and criminality. You even criticized God and blamed Him for having created such a wicked world as earth. You wanted justice and guess what? Just beyond the portal of death you will face perfect and uncompromising justice. The question becomes, "Did you miscalculate? Does God believe in you?"

Wouldn't it be something to stand before an authority you could not lie to? What is this creature that stands before his creator? Here stands a pathological liar. There are more skeletons in the closet than you remembered. How many agonies did you visit upon others? How many did you cheat? How much did you steal? How deep into the pit of deceit did you sink? How many depravities did you embrace? How much did you participate with a gang of thieves who looted and murdered, oh yes, in the name of good? What about your advocacy? We know that you only drove the getaway car. What did you advocate, the murder of babies, a corrupt political system, rigged scales, plundering the treasury, dirty commerce? How many men passed through your bowels?

To stand before the mind of God is something you never anticipated. As you stand in line, you rehearse your defense. You are not guilty because it was just collateral damage, blowback, unintended consequences. Besides, everyone else was doing it, too. You know it's all a lie and you fear like no other fear you ever felt. You stand in a moment of ultimate uncertainty. Your selective memory and crooked representation of yourself will not pass scrutiny and even you know it.

You miscalculated your whole life and now you face perfect, uncompromising justice. The moment is coming where the moral equation will balance. You get to face God with all your felonies.

Chapter 9
The Conditional General Amnesty

Materialism says that the universe is running against the universal gradient of entropy to become evermore complex (evolution). Christian idealism says that entropy was the great curse of God, described in Holy Scripture. He cursed the elements (the ground). Entropy is the law of corruption and points backward in time to a state of perfection. Mankind and all of nature is in a fallen state. Per Pascal, man is a deposed prince who is wretched (unhappy) because he knows he is fallen and must live in his fallenness.

We do not know the crime of the first man and woman but we know that it was so grievous that it brought to Adam and Eve and all their progeny the death penalty. The perfect justice of God required it. When men complain and criticize God for having created such an unjust world of regrets, they are not mindful that we are all on death row awaiting execution. The perfect and uncompromising justice of God has been and will be fully served.

Adam and Eve were exiled into a world of entropy, a prison, a world of toil followed by death and eternal separation from the source of life. What could be worse?

Justice, total, pure and uncompromising justice, gave its verdict; mankind would receive the death penalty. Aside from the sin of Adam and Eve, we have all participated in this sin. We are all culpable. We are all wretched.

God is just but he is also infinitely merciful. There was only one way to satisfy justice and at the same time express infinite mercy. God had to take upon Himself the penalty of death.

God did not create man and then abandon him. God made a plan to reconcile justice and mercy, a plan to restore His creation, a plan to reinstate man to his original glory.

Thus, it is that God would incarnate Himself into human form and suffer the penalty of death. The Holy Scripture says "In the beginning was the word (logos) and the word (logos) became flesh and dwelled upon us." Per theologian Gordon Clark, the Greek word logos could be interpreted as "logic" or "intelligence." Thus we have: "In the beginning was the divine intelligence and the divine intelligence became flesh and dwelled among us." Thus the hidden God revealed Himself and it must be so, for if God did not reveal Himself, man would have no knowledge of God.

Ancient prophecy said that a Holy Messiah (the Anointed One) would come to restore the creation. (The Greek word for "Messiah" is "Christ.") Is it apparent from the record that Christ could have run, he could have changed his mind, but instead he intentionally delivered Himself to be arrested and tried for the crime of blasphemy. He said He was the Messiah and would not retreat from His claim, even in the face of crucifixion. They beat Him but He would not break. They crucified Him and His death was so compelling, the Roman Centurion said "surely this was "the Son (King) of God."

When the Christ took upon Himself the death penalty of man, the Perfect Justice of the law was satisfied. God could now express His mercy and declare a Conditional General Amnesty. The General Amnesty provides forgiveness to anyone who would recognize the divinity of the giver and the wondrous nature of the gift. Anyone who wanted the gift could have a fresh start but they have to recognize the Christ and to live according to the spirit of the fulfilled law; love God with all your heart and soul and mind. Love your neighbor as yourself.

Those were the conditions to participate in a new life, as a new being with the promise that when the creation was fully restored that we would reign with Christ in His spiritual kingdom.

Did He triumph over death as many witnesses said? Or was a resurrection manufactured through legendary accretion? The Holy Messiah gave us great teachings so that we would learn the principles that promote life. However, He was not just a great teacher. He said that He was the Son (King) of God. As Christian writer, C.S. Lewis explains, certain logic flows. He told His disciples that they could stake their eternal souls upon Him. If He was not the Christ, He was a liar and a con man and His teachings were a fraud. What a price He paid to play the part of a would-be Messiah. Crucifixion is gruesome, a death with agony beyond comprehension! His disciples recorded that he delivered Himself to this execution, while they cut and ran. They were afraid they too would be crucified and they wanted no part of it. They feared Roman materialism more than they feared God. He said he would die and rise again from the dead to complete the plan of God. At the moment of truth, facing crucifixion themselves, the disciples fell in line with Roman authority. Jesus went to his crucifixion alone. Nor did He break on the cross. He was who He said He was, even on the cross.

C.S. Lewis provides a second possibility. If Jesus wasn't a con man and a fraud, perhaps he was a lunatic. There are examples of cult leaders who have been able to generate a small following and then lead them into suicide. The question is, who remembers them through the passing of time? Such movements become a forgotten footnote in some old history book. The message of the good news of the risen Christ is 2000 years old and enjoys two billion followers. The best selling book in all of history is the Holy Bible. In all, it is quite a feat for a lunatic. Besides, the disciples knew that there would be a terrible price to pay to persist in this promotion of their Christ. After the charismatic lunatic was dead how did He get his followers to persist in his delusion? What transformed his disciples and gave them courage they did not previously possess?

They said they saw Him risen from the dead. Could this possibly be true? He claimed to be the Messiah but they did not really believe it until He had risen from the dead. The disciples of the

Christ had their own decisions to make. They were liars and con men or they were lunatics or their witness to the risen Christ was true and real.

If they were lunatics and the Christ was dead and gone, it is impossible to explain how a small group of uneducated men with no money or political connections, could launch a world wide religious/philosophical movement. If they were liars and con men, what was their motive? None of them got rich. They established their fame in martyrdom. As soon as the first of them got flogged and executed, the other con men would have abandoned the con. It is impossible to make a convincing case that they were liars and con men. Thieves would cut and run at the first sign of trouble.

They said they saw the risen Christ. They were transformed from cowards to men of the deepest conviction. If one had never seen the sun but rather witnessed only the shining moon, one could reasonably infer the existence of powerful blinding light. The disciples were the shining moon, reflecting the mighty light of the Christ. Let us consider the depth of the conviction of their claim:

- Matthew was killed by a sword wound.
- Mark was dragged to death by horses.
- Luke was hanged.
- John was boiled in oil but survived.
- Peter was crucified upside down.
- James was thrown off a pinnacle.
- James (the greater) was beheaded.

- Bartholomew was flayed to death by a whip.
- Andrew was crucified.
- Thomas was stabbed to death.
- Jude was killed by arrows.
- Matthias was stoned to death.
- Paul was transformed by a vision of Christ, a light from heaven that knocked him off his horse blinding him for three days. According to his own chronicle, Paul had been stoned and left for dead. Five times he was flogged with 39 lashes. Three times he was beaten with rods. He was repeatedly imprisoned. He suffered from hunger, exposure to inclement weather and spent a night and a day in the ocean after a shipwreck. He spent his entire life founding churches and preaching the good news of the Risen Christ. He was tortured and beheaded in Rome for the sake of his Christ. What possibly could drive a man to live such a life if the risen Christ was a lie?

The question is why would all these men risk their lives for a dead man?

The Christ was prophesied from ancient times. He appeared and brought the message of God. He willingly suffered crucifixion, taking on Himself, the death penalty of man. How bad is sin –oh – it's that bad. The Christ changed the course of history and commenced the process for the redemption of mankind and the restoration of the creation. In His resurrection from the dead, He freed mankind from materialist bondage. God offers us a Conditional General Amnesty, forgiveness and redemption if we accept His terms. The restoration of His creation awaits His second coming.

We must acknowledge the identity of the Christ and His payment for our debt. We must enter a guilty plea and express our deep regret for our crimes against the law of God including our crimes against each other. We must acknowledge that our pardon is an expression of God's infinite mercy, paid for by His Christ. We must generate the deepest resolve to turn from materialist bondage and commence a new life, as a new creature. God has promised to help us by the agency of His Holy Spirit.

This is Christian Idealism. It has many enemies and they slander its message. They remember to humanity only the shortcomings of the church and make endless accusations. They mock, endlessly mock. They stood at the foot of the cross and mocked a man being crucified. They mock still. As Joe Sobran says "That the Christ is so hated after 2000 years is astonishing evidence of His identity."

Either there is no God and we live in a material universe or there is God and we live in an ideal universe. We are all materialists or idealists. Materialism offers humanity a short life of cheap thrills followed by eternal death. Death renders life an absurd and meaningless enterprise.

Christian idealism says that God created life and life is eternal. The promise of the Christ is eternal life in His eternal kingdom for those who love God.

Again, we give you Pascal's wager. If the materialist position is correct and the idealist is wrong, then the idealist position is only a delusion among many. Death will swallow it with everything else. On the other hand, if Christian Idealism is right and materialism is wrong, the materialist bears a deep, downside risk as a criminal in rebellion to reality, moral reality, epistemological reality and metaphysical reality. He faces perfect and uncompromising justice without the mercy of the Conditional General Amnesty.

In the end, it is not whether you believe in God, it is whether God believes in you. Therein lies the wager.

Thirteen Books That Will Change Your Life

1. Evolution: A Theory In Crisis - Michael Denton
   ISBN 0-917561-52-X
2. Nature's Destiny – Michael Denton ISBN 0-684-84509-1
3. Darwin's Black Box – Michael Behe ISBN 0-684-82754-9
4. The Real Lincoln – Thomas J. Dilorenzo ISBN 0-7615-3641-8
5. World War I, World War II – Richard Maybury
   ISBN 0-942617-41-X
   ISBN 0-942617-40-X
6. Original Intent – David Barton ISBN 0-925279-75-7
7. America's Real War – Daniel Lapin ISBN 1-57673-366-1
8. Kinsey: Crimes and Consequences – Judith Reisman
   ISBN 0-9666620-1-5
9. Evidence That Demands a Verdict – Josh McDowell
   ISBN 0-7852-4219-8
10. The Case for Christ – Lee Strobel ISBN 0-310-20930-7
11. A Century of War – F. William Engdahl ISBN 3925725199
12. The Politically Incorrect Guide to Darwinism and Intelligent
    Design – Jonathan Wells, Ph.D. ISBN 1-59698-013-3
13. The Politically Incorrect Guide to Christianity – Robert J.
    Hutchinson ISBN 1596985208

About the Author

Allen Michael Green is an independent general securities broker and branch manager. He graduated with honors from Eastern Michigan University where he obtained a Bachelor of Science and Master of Arts Degree. Allen is the founder of A. Green Charity that sponsors A. Green Baseball, a world class youth baseball program. Mr. Green has also sponsored the Ypsilanti Symphony Orchestra and the Greater Ypsilanti Santa Claus Project. He is a civic and business leader in his community.

In 2004, Allen published his first novel, *Blind Baseball: A Father's War* (see www.blindbaseball.com or www.amazon.com), an Orwellian tale of the state sponsored destruction of the family.

Mr. Green enjoys the love of a beautiful wife, two daughters, three stepsons and four wonderful grandchildren.

CPSIA information can be obtained
at www.ICGtesting.com
Printed in the USA
BVHW072221290820
587613BV00002B/129